U0331404

河北省高等院校本土文化英汉双语系列教程

Beautiful
Hebei

美丽河北

燕赵文化概论
（英汉对照）

上册

总 主 编 ◎ 李正栓

本册主编 ◎ 崔　丽　安尚勇

副 主 编 ◎ 霍月红　王　慧　贺宇涛　叶红婷
　　　　　李祯妮　崔伊波　曹佳学　张志新

参编人员 ◎ 朱慧敏　王　雨　纪亚品　白丽伟
　　　　　葛文词　李圣轩　李潇逸　诸怡宁
　　　　　梁　皓　张　枫　赵南南

上海交通大学出版社
SHANGHAI JIAO TONG UNIVERSITY PRESS

内容提要

本教材作为阐述河北省情的双语教材，有助于广大青年学生系统了解河北省的历史传承和风土人情，认识家乡的发展现状，激发学生热爱家乡、报效祖国、服务人民的情感，增强青年学生对家乡的认知度、自豪感、荣誉感和责任感。本教材分上、下两册，包括魅力河北、自然奇观、古城古韵、泥土芬芳、人文胜迹、荣光岁月、百年征程、人杰地灵等八篇内容。本教材可供河北省高等院校各专业开展跨文化课程教学使用。

图书在版编目（CIP）数据

美丽河北. 上册：英汉对照 / 李正栓总主编；崔丽，安尚勇本册主编. — 上海：上海交通大学出版社，2024.3

ISBN 978-7-313-28400-6

Ⅰ.①美⋯ Ⅱ.①李⋯ ②崔⋯ ③安⋯ Ⅲ.①英语–汉语–对照读物 ②河北–概况 Ⅳ.①H319.4：K

中国国家版本馆CIP数据核字〔2023〕第044405号

美丽河北. 上册：英汉对照

MEILI HEBEI. SHANGCE: YINGHAN DUIZHAO

总 主 编：李正栓
本册主编：崔　丽　安尚勇
出版发行：上海交通大学出版社　　　　地　　址：上海市番禺路951号
邮政编码：200030　　　　　　　　　　电　　话：021-64071208
印　　制：常熟市文化印刷有限公司　　经　　销：全国新华书店
开　　本：787mm×1092mm　1/16　　印　　张：15.25
字　　数：319千字
版　　次：2024年3月第1版　　　　　　印　　次：2024年3月第1次印刷
书　　号：ISBN 978-7-313-28400-6
定　　价：59.00元

河北省高等院校本土文化英汉双语系列教程
专家指导委员会

主　任

　　李正栓（河北师范大学）

委　员（以姓氏拼音为序）

　　安尚勇（河北地质大学）

　　崔海英（河北科技师范学院）

　　崔　丽（河北科技大学）

　　高　霄（华北电力大学）

　　杜　磊（河北工程大学）

　　贺宇涛（石家庄学院）

　　黄永亮（河北师范大学）

　　李晓红（华北理工大学）

　　梁小栋（河北中医药大学）

　　王浩勇（河北农业大学）

　　王密卿（河北师范大学）

　　汪艳萍（河北水利电力学院）

　　王显志（华北理工大学）

　　谢　捷（衡水学院）

　　叶慧君（河北大学）

　　张　润（河北经贸大学）

　　张广天（保定学院）

前言

中国位于亚欧大陆东部，太平洋西岸，陆地总面积约 960 万平方千米，居世界第三位。在这雄鸡式的广袤版图中，雪峰皑皑，群山巍峨，高原雄壮，盆地辽阔，丘陵起伏，平原坦荡，戈壁浩瀚，沙漠似海，森林如洋，草原葱郁，河川蜿蜒，峡谷幽深，湖泊晶莹，海域蔚蓝，山河壮丽，景观殊异，美不胜收。5 000 余年的文明，历史悠长，文化璀璨。

河北省拥有约 18.8 万平方千米的陆地面积，位于中国雄鸡版图的胸膛之处。鸟瞰河北大地，北依燕山，南望黄河，西靠太行，东坦沃野，内守京津、外环渤海，其地形走势与整个中国地形特征一致，西北高、东南低，乃华北中心、京畿要地。深厚的文化积淀，浓郁的民风民俗，让河北大地充满了传奇色彩，一代代河北人演绎着"燕赵多有慷慨悲歌之士"的时代传奇。

中国 34 个省级行政区划中，河北省的版图最具趣味，它拱卫着首都北京，并与直辖市天津毗连，京津冀一体难分。然而，在这两大城市的光芒之下，河北省则又是十分低调的——平淡、平凡，以至于谈到河北省，大部分人的脑海中很难有一个清晰的印象。

实际上，河北省，这个中国地貌类型最齐全、自然资源丰富、历史文化深厚的省份，它的精彩之处，出乎人们的意料。

从地形地貌来看，河北省是中国地形地貌最丰富的省份，是一幅亘古至今绵延几千年的美丽画卷。平原广袤，沃野良田；山峦竞秀，小溪潺潺；海浪拍岸，河湖静安；高原揽月，森林无边；草原辽阔，大漠孤烟。从高山到草原再到大海，从山地到平原再到湖泊，这里应有尽有。巍峨太行挺起华夏脊梁，华北平原辽阔坦荡，白洋淀荷红苇绿，碣石外洪波涌起……可以说河北省囊括了中国所有的地质地貌，堪称浓缩的"中国国家地理读本"。

从历史传承来看，河北省是中华文明起源地之一，文化底蕴厚重。神话传说中的盘古开天地、女娲造人、伏羲创八卦都源于此；发现了大量新、旧石器文化遗存的泥河湾被誉为"人类祖先的东方故乡"；黄帝、炎帝、蚩尤在此逐鹿从征战到融合，开创了华夏 5 000 余年文明史；大禹划分九州，河北省地属冀州，被誉为希望之地；春秋战国时期，河北省分属燕、赵两国，故而这片土地在后世被称为"燕赵大地"；元、明、清三朝定都北京，河北省成为拱卫京城的畿辅重地；革命战争年代，河北省是重要的对敌战场和革命根据地；西柏坡是中共中央最后一个农村指挥所，1949 年 3 月 23 日，中国共产党从这里赴京开创"建国大业"，被誉为"新中国从这里走来"。

新中国成立之后的河北省，人民自力更生、艰苦奋斗，战胜洪涝、地震、干旱等重大自然灾害，为河北经济社会发展、人民生活富裕奠定了坚实基础。改革开放后，河北人民不断解放思想，大胆开拓创新，取得辉煌成就，燕赵大地焕发出前所未有的生机与活力。

进入到 21 世纪，京津冀协同发展、千年大计雄安新区规划建设、与北京共同举办第 24 届冬奥会这三件大事，更为河北省的发展提供了千载难逢的历史机遇。

回顾光辉历程我们无比自豪，展望光明前景我们信心满怀，在全面建设社会主义现代化国家新征程上，河北人民不忘初心、牢记使命、不懈奋斗、不断开创新时代。

这片土地蕴含的时光如此悠长，让人敬畏！

这片土地的自然景观如此妖娆，让人热爱！

这片土地就是我们的家乡——美丽河北！

"为什么我的眼里常含泪水？因为我对这土地爱得深沉……"

知来处，明事理，爱祖国，爱家乡。我们对家乡的热爱之情不是自发产生的，是基于对家乡的了解和认识不断形成的。习近平总书记在《知之深　爱之切》一书中写道："要热爱自己的家乡，首先要了解家乡。深厚的感情必须以深刻的认识作基础。唯有对家乡知之甚深，才能爱之愈切。"

出于对家乡的热爱之情，也出于作为教育工作者的责任与担当，我们以教育部印发的《高等学校课程思政建设指导纲要》及"三进"教育要求为指导，结合我国高校大学英语教学实际情况，组织河北部分高校教师编写了这套涵盖河北省情的英汉双语教材，取名《美丽河北》，供河北省高等学校学生使用。

省情教育是国情教育的重要基础和组成部分，是国情教育地方化的体现，也是爱国主

义教育的重要内容,对于深入开展青年学生思想政治和德育教育工作,将会发挥重要作用。

本教材作为介绍河北省情内容的双语教材,有助于广大青年学生系统了解河北省的历史传承、风土人情,认识家乡的发展现状,激发学生热爱家乡、报效祖国、服务人民的情感,增强青年学生对家乡的认知度、自豪感、荣誉感和责任感。中国共产党第二十次全国代表大会报告中提出科教兴国,再次强调了教育的重要性,党之大计的根本是教育,教育关乎民生、关乎国家的发展。我们编写这套教材也是落实党的二十大要求,将价值塑造、知识传授和能力培养融为一体,通过双语教学的形式,把自信、开放、创新的意识融入学生的灵魂,教育引导他们了解河北、热爱河北、对外宣传河北,激励他们为建设新河北而勤奋学习、建功立业,成为激发大学生热爱家乡、建设家园、报效祖国的动力源泉。

本教材分上、下两册,包括魅力河北、自然奇观、古城古韵、泥土芬芳、人文胜迹、荣光岁月、百年征程、人杰地灵等八篇。在这八篇中,我们编写的内容虽不能面面俱到,但也尽可能做到提纲挈领,以点带面,突出有关河北省情的重要知识内容。

本教材信息量大,为帮助学习者顺利学习,我们采用前半部分英文、后半部分中文的排版模式。在英文部分,每篇起始处设置课前导读,每篇结尾处设置练习题,增加学习者的学习印象。教材最后设有附录,弥补自然奇观、古城古韵、泥土芬芳、人文胜迹、荣光岁月等篇章中未曾提到的大量相关信息。本教材可供河北省高等院校各专业开展跨文化课程教学使用。

非常感谢参与编写工作的各位高校教师,有了他们辛勤的付出与无私的支持,这套教材才能展现在大家面前。谨以此书献给伟大的祖国!献给美丽的河北!献给可爱可敬的教育工作者!

中国文化博大精神,河北文化厚重悠长,然而编者水平有限,错误与不当之处在所难免,敬请读者和专家不吝赐教。

本教材编写委员会

2023 年 4 月

Contents

English Section
Part One   Charming Hebei, The Land of Yan-Zhao

Chapter 1   The Geographical Features of Hebei   —004

—Leaning Against the Taihang Mountains and Bordering the Bohai Sea, Taking the Yanshan Mountains as Its Barrier and Overlooking the Fertile Plain

Chapter 2   The Historical Development of Hebei   —008

—Changes from the Ancient Jizhou to the Important Region of the Capital and Its Environs

Chapter 3   The Climatic Characteristics of Hebei   —015

—Distinct in Four Seasons and Abundant in Natural Resources

Chapter 4   The Transport Network in Hebei   —021

—An Outlet Toward the East, a Connecting Point Toward the West, and an Integral Part of Beijing-Tianjin-Hebei Transport Integration

Chapter 5   The Cultural Characteristics of Hebei   —026

—Yan-Zhao Culture Overlapped with the Culture of the Capital and Its Environs

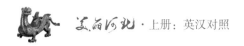

Part Two　Wonders of Nature: The Beauty of Mountains and Rivers

Chapter 6　Beidaihe　　　　　　　　　　　　　　　　　　　　　　　−038

—A Popular Resort to Embrace Cool and Comfortable Summer with Blue Sea and Golden Beach

Chapter 7　Mount Wuling　　　　　　　　　　　　　　　　　　　　　−044

—A Sacred Buddhist Cultural Mountain, A Summer Resort of Deep Enchantment

Chapter 8　Yesanpo　　　　　　　　　　　　　　　　　　　　　　　−049

—Treasure House of North China Canyon

Chapter 9　Zhangshiyan　　　　　　　　　　　　　　　　　　　　　−055

—Three Ancient Roads Connecting Nine Valleys, Eight Spots Hidden in Four Scenic Areas

Chapter 10　Hengshui Lake　　　　　　　　　　　　　　　　　　　−060

—Yan-Zhao's Most Beautiful Wetland, a Paradise for Birds

Chapter 11　Bashang Grasslands　　　　　　　　　　　　　　　　−064

—The World of Grass and the Ocean of Flowers

Part Three　Ancient Cities with Picturesque Views

Chapter 12　Chengde　　　　　　　　　　　　　　　　　　　　　　−072

—The Summer Resort and Hunting Ground of the Qing Dynasty Royals

Chapter 13　Baoding　　　　　　　　　　　　　　　　　　　　　　−077

—The Southern Gate of China's Capital City Beijing

Chapter 14   Zhengding   —083

　　—A Thousand-Year-Old County in the Modern Times

Chapter 15   Shanhaiguan Pass   —089

　　—The First Pass under Heaven

Chapter 16   Handan   —094

　　—A City with a History of 3,000 Years

Chapter 17   Yuxian County   —099

　　—"The Ancient Architecture Museum" of Hebei

Part Four   Intangible Cultural Heritages Nurtured in This Fragrant Land

Chapter 18   Yuxian County Paper−Cutting   —106

　　—The Soulful Flowers Blooming on this Ancient Land

Chapter 19   Hengshui Interior Painting   —109

　　—Miraculous Craftsmanship Inside a Small Bottle

Chapter 20   Anguo Medicinal Materials   —113

　　—The Charm of the Millennium Medicine Capital

Chapter 21   Shadow Puppetry   —116

　　—A Myriad of Life Stories under the Light and Shadow

Chapter 22   Cangzhou Martial Arts   —120

　　—The Hometown of Chinese Martial Arts

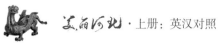
Chapter 23 Wuqiao Acrobatics ──123

　　──The Cradle of Chinese Acrobatics

Chapter 24 Quyang Stone Carving ──125

　　──An Unparalleled Beauty Crafted Through Two Thousand Years of Hammering and Chiseling

Chapter 25 Jingxing Lahua ──129

　　──A Graceful and Well-proportioned Folk Dance Art

Chapter 26 Hebei Bangzi ──132

　　──A Melody Lingering in the Land of Yan-Zhao

中文部分
第1篇　魅力河北　燕赵大地

第1章　河北的地理特征 ──138

　　──倚太行临渤海，屏燕山俯沃野

第2章　河北的历史沿革 ──140

　　──从古冀州到京畿重地的变迁

第3章　河北的气候特征 ──143

　　──四季分明，物产丰富

第4章　河北的交通网络 ──147

　　──东出西联，京津冀交通一体化

第5章　河北的文化特征 ──150

　　──相互重叠的燕赵文化与京畿文化

第2篇　自然奇观　山川之美

第6章　北戴河 ──156

　　──碧海金沙滩，消暑绝胜地

第 7 章　雾灵山　　　　　　　　　　　　　　　　　　　　—159

————求道灵山，避暑凉岛

第 8 章　野三坡　　　　　　　　　　　　　　　　　　　　—162

————华北峡谷珍品

第 9 章　嶂石岩　　　　　　　　　　　　　　　　　　　　—165

————三栈牵九套，四屏藏八景

第 10 章　衡水湖　　　　　　　　　　　　　　　　　　　—168

————燕赵最美湿地，鸟类天堂

第 11 章　坝上草原　　　　　　　　　　　　　　　　　　—170

————草的世界，花的海洋

第3篇　古城古韵　名城之美

第 12 章　承德　　　　　　　　　　　　　　　　　　　　—174

————清代皇家的避暑围猎之地

第 13 章　保定　　　　　　　　　　　　　　　　　　　　—177

————首都北京的南大门

第 14 章　正定　　　　　　　　　　　　　　　　　　　　—180

————千年古郡沐新风

第 15 章　山海关　　　　　　　　　　　　　　　　　　　—183

————天下第一关

第 16 章　邯郸　　　　　　　　　　　　　　　　　　　　—186

————一座等了你三千年的城

第 17 章　蔚县　　　　　　　　　　　　　　　　　　　　—188

————河北省的古建筑博物馆

第4篇　泥土芬芳　非遗之美

第 18 章　蔚县剪纸　　　　　　　　　　　　　　　　　　—192

————古老土地上的灵魂之花

第 19 章　衡水内画 —194

　　　　——寸天厘地，鬼斧神工

第 20 章　安国药材 —196

　　　　——千年药都的魅力

第 21 章　皮影 —198

　　　　——灯影下的百态人生

第 22 章　沧州武术 —200

　　　　——武健泱泱乎有表海雄风

第 23 章　吴桥杂技 —202

　　　　——没有吴桥不成班

第 24 章　曲阳石雕 —204

　　　　——一锤千年尽显绝代风华

第 25 章　井陉拉花 —206

　　　　——舞姿健美，舒展有方

第 26 章　河北梆子 —208

　　　　——燕赵大地的宫商正韵

附录 —211

附录 1　河北省行政区划名录 —212

附录 2　河北省森林公园、地质公园和风景名胜区名录 —214

附录 3　河北省国家级非物质文化遗产名录 —217

附录 4　河北省历史文化名城名镇名村名录 —224

参考文献 —227

English Section

Part One
Charming Hebei, The Land of Yan-Zhao

According to the description of Hebei in *Jifu Tongzhi* (《畿辅通志》) (a book of comprehensive records of Hebei) compiled during the reign of Emperor Kangxi of the Qing Dynasty, "In Hebei, there are the precipitous Taihang Mountains, the roaring Hunhe River, the vast plains and magnificent hills, the strategically important military forts such as Lulong and Diao E, the Juyong Pass serving as a protection in the south, and the Dushi Pass serving as a barrier in the north. The land here produces millet, beans and other crops, and the rivers and lakes here provide fish and salt. The local people still maintain the temperament of 'passionate and tragic heroism.'" Hebei got its name because it is located to the north of the lower reaches of the Yellow River. "He" here refers to the Yellow River, and "bei" means "to the north of". Compared with other provinces of China, its geographical location is quite unique in that it encircles Beijing and Tianjin, which on the one hand weakens the integrity of the spatial connection within Hebei, and on the other hand, it creates the close relationship between Beijing, Tianjin and Hebei. In terms of transportation, as it is located in the eastern part of China, it has the location advantage of serving as "an outlet toward the east, and a connecting point toward the west", and it is also the province that must be passed to connect the capital and the other parts of China in land transportation; in terms of culture, Hebei presents the overlapping characteristics of the culture of Yan-Zhao and the culture of the capital and its surrounding areas, with both the temperament

of the "passionate and tragic heroism" of the ancient people and the spirit of selfless dedication of modern people.

Lead-in Questions

(1) Please talk about the image of Hebei in your mind before reading this division.

(2) How much do you know about the geography and topography of Hebei? Please discuss them with your classmates.

(3) What role has Hebei played in the long history of China? How has its role changed in history?

(4) Please use one sentence to describe the humanistic characteristics of Hebei.

◫ Chapter 1
The Geographical Features of Hebei

—Leaning Against the Taihang Mountains and Bordering the Bohai Sea, Taking the Yanshan Mountains as Its Barrier and Overlooking the Fertile Plain

Hebei is located at the intersection of east longitude 113°27′ to 119°50′ and north latitude 36°03′ to 42°37′. It is 730 kilometers long from north to south and 560 kilometers wide from east to west. Located in the hinterland of North China, it covers an area of 188,800 square kilometers, with the Bohai Sea on the east, the Taihang Mountains in the west, the Yanshan Mountains in the

Harvest grain from wheat fields in Handan, Hebei
河北邯郸 麦田收粮

north and through which it spreads into the Inner Mongolia Plateau, and the Hebei Plain in the middle. It surrounds Beijing and Tianjin, the two municipalities directly under the Central Government, bordering Shandong Province and Henan Province on the southeast and south, Shanxi Province across the Taihang Mountains on the west, Inner Mongolia Autonomous Region on the northwest and Liaoning Province on the northeast. It contains 11 prefecture-level cities, including Shijiazhuang, Tangshan, Handan, Baoding, Cangzhou, Langfang, Hengshui, Xingtai, Zhangjiakou, Chengde, and Qinghuangdao, of which Shijiazhuang is its provincial capital city.

Geographically, Hebei is located in the southern margin of the Inner Mongolia geosyncline and the north of Sino-Korean paraplatform. As to its terrain, the Bashang Plateau, which belongs to the southern margin of the Inner Mongolia Plateau, is in the north of Hebei, and the Yanshan Mountains and the Taihang Mountains form a semi-ring, encircling the Hebei Plain, which is on the south of the Yanshan Mountains and on the east of the Taihang Mountains. With a bird's-eye view, Hebei's terrain is in consistent with the terrain features of China, high in the northwest and low in the southeast, generally presenting a distinct three-step structure. The maximum difference in altitude in Hebei is more than 2,500 meters, with a wide variety of landforms, each of which has its own distinctive features, such as high mountains, basins, undulating plateau and hills, vast plain, low-lying lands and mixtures of them.

The northwest Bashang Plateau covers an area of 160,000 square kilometers, accounting for 8.5% of the total surface area of the whole province. It is adjacent to the Inner Mongolia Plateau, with an average altitude of 1,200−1,500 meters above sea level. The terrain is high with little undulation, thus presenting a scene that it looks like "a mountain when seen from a long distance, but a plain when seen from a short distance". There are many lakes, mires, shoals, ridges and vast natural grassland on the plateau.

The mountainous areas in Hebei mainly consist of the Yanshan Mountains and the Taihang Mountains, with the total area of about 90,100 square kilometers and accounting for 48.1% of the total surface area of the province, if the areas of hills and inter-mountain basins are included.

The Yanshan Mountains lies in the north of Hebei, extending from east to west. The rocks here are diverse and complex, forming various types of mountainous landforms, as well as picturesque peaks and strangely shaped stones. It is also the origins of the Luanhe River, the Chaobai River and the other rivers. The Taihang Mountains lies in the west of Hebei, with its main part extending from northeast to southwest. It is the natural boundary between Hebei Province and Shanxi Province. The landforms of this area vary widely due to the complex geological conditions of the Taihang Mountains. The elevation of its main range is 1,000−1,500 meters, and Xiaowutai Mountain, the highest peak in Hebei, located at the north end of the Taihang Mountains, is at an elevation of 2,882 meters.

The plain on the east of the Taihang Mountains and on the south of the Yanshan Mountains is a part of the North China Plain. It covers a total area of about 81,600 square kilometers, accounting for 43.4% of the total surface area of the province. The altitude of the plain is not high, mostly below 100 meters, and most parts are less than 50 meters above sea level. The low-lying lands scattered on the plain cover a total area of 1,000 square meters, with their central area between Baoding, a city of Hebei and Dagu, an area in Tianjin. The well-known Baiyangdian Lake, Wen'anwa and Dawa are located in this area.

There are many rivers in Hebei, of which more than 300 rivers measure between 18 kilometers and 1,000 kilometers. Most rivers in the territory of Hebei originate from or flow through the Yanshan Mountains, the northern mountainous area and the Taihang Mountains. Because of the terrain, some of their downstream tributaries merge into the sea or flow into the sea alone, while others flow into inland lakes. From south to north, the main rivers are as follows: Zhangweinan Canal, Ziya River, Daqing River, Yongding River, Chaobai River, Jiyun River, Luanhe River, Yinhe River, Wuladai River, Laoha River, etc. They respectively belong to five major river systems of Haihe River, Luanhe River, Neilu River, Liaohe River and the small coastal river system.

The mainland coastline all over China stretches nearly 20,000 kilometers. In contrast, the length of the 487-kilometer coastline in Hebei is not prominent indeed. However, along the coastline under the jurisdiction of Hebei, there are many ports and coastal industrial parks in cities of Qinhuangdao, Tangshan, Cangzhou and so on. From north to south, the ports are Qinghuangdao Port, Tangshan Port (including Jingtang Port and Caofeidian Port), and Huanghua Port, and each of them has its own features. As the "hub of north-to-south coal trans-shipment", Qinghuangdao Port has been transformed and is developing container transportation and cruise home-port; Tangshan Port is a bridgehead opening up to Northeast Asia. It is being developed into a major hub of crude energy materials to serve the national strategy of China; Huanghua Port connects the six cities in central Hebei, and it is the most convenient port for Xiong'an New Area.

Hebei has unique natural resources endowment, and is the only province in China with diverse landforms, including plateau, mountains, hills, deserts, basins, plain, rivers, lakes and coast. The terrain of Hebei is described as "sickle-like mountain ranges, fan-like rivers, carpet-like plain, and plate-like sea". It is honored as the landform "museum" of China, as well as the "miniature of China's geography".

Rare Tree Grassland in Fengning County, Chengde City
承德市丰宁县稀树草原

Chapter 2
The Historical Development of Hebei

—Changes from the Ancient Jizhou to the Important Region of the Capital and Its Environs

Jizhou is one of the nine states (administrative regions) of the Han nationality area described in *Yu Gong* (《禹贡》), which is one of the chapters of the Chinese classic, *The Book of History*. According to this book, Yu the Great[①] divided the whole nation into nine states, among which Jizhou ranked first, including today's Beijing City, Tianjin City, Hebei Province, Shanxi Province, the north part of Henan Province, as well as some regions of Liaoning Province and Inner Mongolia Autonomous Region.

The name "Hebei" originates from "Hebei Dao"[②] (河北道) in Tang Dynasty. "Yan-Zhao", another name referring to Hebei, dates back to an earlier time, the Pre-Qin Period.

Since the Spring and Autumn Period and the Warring States Period when a hundred schools of thought argued against each other, the China's regional cultural pattern has been established as follows: "Yan-Zhao" has become a name for Hebei (today's Beijing, Tianjin and Hebei Province), "Qilu" for Shandong Province, "Wuyue" for the two provinces of Jiangsu and Zhejiang, "Sanjin" for Shanxi Province, "Sanqin" for Shaanxi Province, "Bashu" for Sichuan Province and Chongqing. All these names used today originate from the names of the ancient states at that time.

During the Spring and Autumn Period, Hebei was the battlefield for Yan State and Zhao State to contend for hegemony. Jin State, the strongest state in the north at that time, was divided up by the other three states of Han, Zhao and Wei. Zhao originally chose Jinyang (today's Taiyuan, Shanxi), a place in the basin of the Loess Plateau, as its capital city, then it moved its capital to Handan, which is in the plain of Hebei. In its peak time, the territory of Zhao was

---

① Yu the Great: also known as Da Yu, an ancient hero in prehistoric times.
② Hebei Dao: Dao is a term of administrative division, which is equivalent to a present-day province in the Tang Dynasty and below the provincial level in the Qing Dynasty and the early years of the Republic of China.

much larger than today's Hebei Province, with its hinterland in the central and southern parts of today's Hebei. The northern part of today's Hebei, Beijing and Tianjin were owned by Yan State at that time. Thus the so-called "land of Yan-Zhao", which includes Beijing and Tianjin, actually covers bigger areas than today's Hebei Province.

After the Qin Dynasty unified China in 221 B. C., it adopted the "prefectures and counties system", and in today's Hebei, it set up eight prefectures one after another, namely, Shanggu, Yuyang, Youbeiping, Guangyang, Handan, Julu, Dai and Hengshan.

From the Han Dynasty to the Sui Dynasty, this area was divided into two parts, namely Youzhou and Jizhou[①]. The southwest of Youzhou and the whole Jizhou covered today's Hebei Province.

In the Tang Dynasty, Hebei Dao was established, which covered the basic area of today's Hebei Province, and it is also the origin of the present name of Hebei Province.

In the Song and Jin Dynasties, Hebei Dao was changed into Hebei Lu[②], which was divided into Hebei West Lu and Hebei East Lu later.

During the Yuan, Ming and Qing Dynasties, Hebei, as the heart of China at that time, covered the capital city and its surrounding areas. In the Ming Dynasty, North Zhili Province was established on the basis of Hebei Lu in the Yuan Dynasty, which laid the foundation of the territory of today's Hebei Province. In the Qing Dynasty, Zhili Province replaced the name of North Zhili Province, and its territory also changed slightly.

In modern times, the territory of Hebei has changed frequently, but there is no big change on the whole, and eventually it becomes what it is today.

The territories of Hebei have been changed frequently from the hinterland of Yan-Zhao during the Warring States Period to today's Hebei, while the vast plain located on the southeast of the Taihang Mountains and the south of the Yanshan Mountains has always been its core region. The part of the North China Plain within Hebei is generally called the Hebei

---

① Youzhou and Jizhou: Zhou is a term of administrative division, the area of which varies in size in different dynasties
② Hebei Lu: Lu is a term of administrative division used in the Song and Jin Dynasties

Plain. It is also called the Haihe River Plain, because it is mainly located in the basin of Haihe River.

The North China Plain is one of the important birthplaces and breeding places of Chinese civilization, and also the economic and cultural center before the Song Dynasty. Hebei is an indispensable part of it.

Hebei takes the Yanshan Mountains as its natural barrier in the north, and leans against the Taihang Mountains in the west. The ridges of these two mountains and the plain form the shape of a huge inverted "L" or a counterclockwise rotated "J", which is the outline of the terrain of Hebei.

The Hebei Plain is a part of the Central Plains (comprising the middle and lower reaches of the Yellow River). The mountainous region in the north of Hebei was once a zone where agricultural civilization and nomadic civilization interlocked and intermingled with each other. The Yanshan Mountains and the Taihang Mountains are like two barriers, which were taken as the natural "Great Wall" and were heavily relied on by all the rulers of the successive dynasties. The southern part of Hebei, which has long been the area in northern China with the most glorious history and culture, and the most developed economy, is the key part of the hinterland of the Central Plains, which constitutes the vast and fertile North China Plain together with Henan Province and Shandong Province.

The Haihe River, the "mother river" of Beijing, Tianjin and Hebei, is a huge river system. It consists of five tributaries, i.e., the Chaobai River, the Yongding River, the Daqing River, the Ziya River and the South Canal. They converge at the Sancha River Estuary in Tianjin and then flow into the Haihe River. The Haihe River basin is shaped just like a big fan.

The middle and upper reaches of the Haihe River had already created many brilliant achievements during the 3,000 to 4,000 years before Tianjin became prominent on the stage of history. The Haihe River basin gave birth to many ancient cities, such as Anyang, Handan, Datong, Zhangjiakou and some cities around Shijiazhuang, such as Lingshou, Zhengding, Dingzhou and so on. Each of them boasts a history of 2,000 to 3,000 years.

The cities along the east foot of the Taihang Mountains in Hebei joined into a line, forming a civilization corridor and a city zone in the alluvial fan of the Haihe River. This line is also a part of the so called "north-south road".

Whether the northern cities such as Chang'an, Luoyang and Kaifeng, which were to communicate with the south, or the southern cities such as Hangzhou and Nanjing, which hoped to exchange with the north, they all had to pass this road at the east foot of the Taihang Mountains. Today's Beijing-Guangzhou Railway is the modern version of this road, and almost all the important cities in China from south to north are on this road.

At least since the Spring and Autumn Period and the Warring States Period, a smooth north-south road had been formed between Ji (today's Beijing) , an important town in Yan State, and Yin (today's Anyang), an ancient capital city seated in the Central Plains. After defeating the other six states, Qin Shi Huang, the first Emperor of China, ordered all the vehicle should have the same width between their wheels and built a network of roads, one of which connected today's Beijing and Anyang. The highways developed on the basis of this ancient road now consist of the Beijing-Shijiazhuang Highway and the Shijiazhuang-Anyang Highway, both being the northern section of today's Beijing-Hong Kong&Macao Expressway. And both the Beijing-Hankou Railway and the Beijing-Guangzhou Railway run through this ancient traffic artery.

Along this road, many ancient cities, which were taken as capitals in history, are distributed in the regions of today's Hebei and Beijing: the capital city of the Shang Dynasty, Xing (today's Xingtai, Hebei); the capital city of the Yan State, Xiadu (today's Yixian County, Baoding, Hebei), the capital city of Zhongshan State (today's Lingshou County, Shijiazhuang, Hebei and Dingzhou, Baoding, Hebei), and the capital city of Zhao State (today's Handan, Hebei) during the Spring and Autumn Period and the Warring States Period; the capital city from the late Wei Dynasty of the Three Kingdoms Period to the Northern Dynasties, Yecheng (located in the west to today's Linzhang County, Handan, Hebei); the capital city of Liao, Song, Jin, Yuan, Ming and Qing Dynasties, Beijing. Among them, Yecheng, which was once in the south of today's Handan, is honored as a minor "capital of six dynasties", because it was once taken as the capital city successively by six states from the Three Kingdoms Period to the Northern Dynasties. With the fall of the Northern Qi Dynasty of the Northern Dynasties, Yecheng turned into ruins, and its

culture began to move to a city on the south bank of the Zhanghe River, Anyang, which is exactly the southern end point of this road.

From the Warring States Period to the Han Dynasty, the capitals of Yan State and Zhao State, which were two of the seven powers, as well as the capital of Zhongshan State, a second-tier state during that period, were all located in Hebei; in the article of *Biographies of Extremely Wealthy Businessmen* collected in *Historical Records*, the famous historian Sima Qian mentioned that from the Warring States Period to the Western Han Dynasty there were nine economic "metropolises", and two of them, Ji and Handan, were in today's Beijing-Tianjin-Hebei region. Both of them were as important as today's national central cities.

From the Three Kingdoms Period to the Northern Dynasties, Yecheng, which was located in the south of Hebei, was successively taken as the capital city of six states during that period full of frequent wars. When Chang'an and Luoyang were destroyed in the wars, Yecheng became an northern economic center with temporary peace in that troubled times. The ruins of this ancient city and the related cultural relics excavated in Yecheng proved that it was once a metropolis of economic prosperity and cultural inclusiveness.

"Bronze Sparrow Terrace" mentioned in the poem by Cao Cao, one famous warlord of the Three Kingdoms Period, was the well-known landmark building of Yecheng.

Handan Bronze Sparrow Terrace
邯郸 铜雀台

In Sui and Tang Dynasties, there was no capital city in Hebei, but it was still an economically developed area. Moreover, besides the existing "north-south road" at the east foot of the Taihang Mountains, a new canal, a transportation artery that served as the "national corridor" at that time, was opened up. This is the grand canal that connected Youzhou (today's Beijing) and Beizhou (today's Qinghe County, Xingtai, Hebei).

After that, the role of Hebei has changed, but it is still important. Its leading role on the historical stage has been replaced by Beijing, which was once a part of Hebei. When talking about Hebei, people usually separate it from Beijing, which is an improper understanding, because Beijing and Hebei are one as a whole whether from the perspective of geography or culture.

Before the mid-ancient times[1], Hebei didn't have any ecological and environmental problem as today. With great economic potential, while providing "blood" to Chang'an and Luoyang, Hebei itself was still very rich. In addition to its economic achievements, Hebei had also given birth to numerous talents. Daming Prefecture (in today's Daming County, Handan), which was the northern second capital of the Northern Song Dynasty, stands for the last glamour in the list of capital cities in Hebei. Afterwards, Beijing (as a part of Yan-Zhao cultural area) began to enjoy the glory as a capital city. It was called Nanjing in the Liao Dynasty, Zhongdu in the Jin Dynasty, Dadu in the Yuan Dynasty, and Beijing in the Ming and Qing Dynasties.

Before the Song Dynasty, the Hebei Plain was an important economic and cultural center, which gave birth to a large number of influential talents from generation to generation. Its economy and culture were both very prosperous. After the Song Dynasty, Hebei mainly served as a region of great political and military importance and the most important frontier of Beijing. And since then, the once glorious "south-north road" at the east foot of the Taihang Mountains only played the role of a transportation corridor economically. From the Song Dynasty to the modern times, Hebei's territory has changed many times, its name has changed back and forth between Zhili and Hebei, and its provincial capital city has

---

[1] the mid-ancient times: the period from the Northern and Southern Dynasties to the Ming Dynasty is called the mid-ancient times of China.

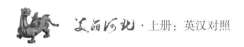

been moved many times among the three cities: Tianjin, Baoding and Shijiazhuang.

From being sonorous, being melodious, to finally being gentle, the history of Yan-Zhao is like a beautiful song. The enduring temperament of "passionate and tragic heroism" together with the strong sense of righteousness has lasted for thousands of years in this land. Such a melody has already internalized itself in this land and will still echo in the hearts of Hebei people.

Panorama of Guangfu Ancient City, Handan
邯郸市广府古城全景

Chapter 3
The Climatic Characteristics of Hebei
—Distinct in Four Seasons and Abundant in Natural Resources

Hebei is located on the eastern coast of the Eurasian continent in the mid-latitude, and belongs to the temperate semi-humid and semi-arid continental monsoon climate. Most of the region has four distinct seasons with great disparity between summer and winter. It also has distinct wet and dry seasons. The climate of Hebei is characterized by cold and dry winter

Caofeidian Wetland
曹妃甸湿地

with little rain and snow, dry and windy spring with great temperature difference; hot summer with concentrated rainfall, and pleasantly cool and sunny autumn with little rain. In general, Hebei has good climatic conditions, with comfortable temperature and abundant sunshine and heat from the sunlight. The rainfall and sunlight heat are synchronized, which is suitable for the growth of various crops, forests and fruits.

The annual average temperature in Hebei rises gradually from north to south. The annual average temperature of the northern plateau is lower than 4 °C, with the lowest average temperature of −0.3 °C in Yudaokou (a town of Chengde City). In the south-central region, the annual average temperature rises above 12 °C, with the highest average temperature of 14 °C in the Fengfeng Mining District of Handan City. There is a great annual average temperature difference between the south and the north of Hebei. The annual extreme high temperatures in Hebei often occur in June, which can reach above 40 °C to the south of the Great Wall. There are 18−25 sweltering hot days with temperatures above 35 °C in the southern plain, and 10−18 such days in the central plain and the southern mountainous areas of the Taihang Mountains, while only 1−4 such days in the coastal and northern mountainous areas of Tangshan and Qinhuangdao. There is no such sweltering weather in the north plateau, and the annual extremely low temperatures are mainly there, which can reach temperatures below −30 °C.

Hebei is rich in different types of wetland resources, including shallow seas, mudflats, rivers, reservoirs, lakes and low-lying lands. All of them have important values in resources, climate and scientific research. The wetland area accounts for 59% of the total land area of Hebei, which is one time higher than the national average level of 27%. The wetlands are mainly distributed in the coastal area and the Bashang Plateau, while only a small amount of wetlands scatter in the plain and vast mountainous areas. Among them, Changli Gold Coast Wetland, Luanhe Estuary Wetland, Baiyangdian Wetland, Beidaihe Coastal Wetland, Cangzhou Nandagang Wetland, Zhangjiakou Bashang Wetland (at Angulinao in Zhangbei County) and Hengshui Lake Wetland are listed in "The List of Important Wetlands in China" issued by the State Forestry Administration. The various types of wetlands and plant communities provide suitable

habitats for wild animals of different ecological types. At the same time, these wetlands also serve as habitats for many migrating birds to rest and replenish their energy on their way.

The geological conditions in Hebei are particularly conductive to the formation of minerals, so it is relatively rich in mineral resources. Now there are 159 kinds of discovered minerals, and 133 kinds of minerals with proved reserves, among which 39 kinds are among the top six in the provinces of Chinese mainland by their reserves. Staple minerals such as coal, iron, oil (natural gas), gold and various kinds of limestone are the dominant minerals in Hebei. The coal production in Hebei ranks third in China. It has a variety of coal, with coking coal as the main kind. The coal is mainly distributed in Tangshan, Handan, Xingtai, Zhangjiakou and so on. The iron mine is mainly distributed in the mountainous areas of the Taihang Mountains and the Yanshan Mountains, whose proved reserves rank third in China, and they are well combined with metallurgical auxiliary raw materials. Hebei is also one of the six major gold mine concentrated distribution areas in China, and its gold output ranks third in China, with Chengde as the main production area. Oil and natural gas resources are mainly distributed in the central and eastern parts of the

Hebei Plain and the coastal areas of eastern areas. In addition, limestone mineral resources are abundant, diverse, and of high-quality in Hebei.

In terms of new energy, geothermal resources are mostly concentrated in the central and northern areas of Hebei, where the total amount that can be mined is equivalent to 11.05 billion tons of standard coal, ranking third in China after Xizang and Yunnan. The medium and low temperature thermal groundwater resources in Hebei rank first in China. There are 241 places of thermal groundwater with development value in Hebei. Among them, 92 places are in the mountainous areas with the average water temperature of 40−70 °C, while the rest are distributed in the plains with the highest water temperature of 95−118 °C. There's a great disparity in regional distribution of wind energy resources with obvious seasonal change. Wind energy resources are rich in the Bashang Plateau and some narrow coastal areas in Hebei, while the vast mountainous areas and most parts of the Hebei Plain are short of wind energy resources. The solar energy resources of Hebei are next only to that of Qinghai- Xizang and Northwest China, with an annual radiation quantity of 4,981−5,966 MJ/m^2. The annual sunshine hours in Zhangjiakou, Chengde and the east of Cangzhou are 2,800−3,000 hours, making them the regions which enjoy the longest sunshine hours in Hebei. The annual sunshine duration in Xingtai, and the western and central part of Handan is 2,500−2,600 hours, making them the regions with the shortest sunshine hours in Hebei. The annual sunshine duration in most other areas is 2,600−2,750 hours, with the percentage of bright sunshine of 50%−70%.

Hebei is relatively rich in animal resources. There are more than 530 species of terrestrial vertebrates (including amphibians) in Hebei, accounting for about 29.0% of those in China. Among them, there are nearly 80 species of beasts, accounting for 21.5% of those in China. And there are more than 420 species of birds in Hebei, accounting for 36.1% of the total species in China, including many precious and rare species, such as brown-eared pheasants, white-crowned long-tailed pheasants and swans. Among them, brown-eared pheasants are a kind of rare animal that is only found in Hebei and Shanxi. There are 19 species of reptiles and 10 species of amphibians, including one of the national first-class protected animals in China (i.e. North China leopard). There are more than 100 species of livestock and poultry in Hebei, many of which are superior breeds well-known both inside and outside Hebei, such as Zhangbei Horse, Yangyuan Donkey, Zhangjiakou Red Steppe, Wu'an Goat, Jinan Cattle and Shenzhou Pig. There are more than 110 kinds of fish along the coast of Hebei, the main kinds including hairtail, yellow croaker, barracuda, flatfish, flounder, pomfret, and the most famous sweetfish. The cephalochordate lancelet in Qinhuangdao is among the list of the second-class protected animals in China. There are more than 20 kinds of marine shrimp, including the most famous prawn and the most productive flat lobster. And there are more than 10 kinds of crabs. The main shellfishes are Meretrix Lusoria, Cyclina sinensis, razor clam, blood clam and oyster, etc. Sea cucumbers, which belongs to the echinoderm family, also have a certain output. The area of freshwater in Hebei covers about 1.2 million *mu* (*mu* is a Chinese unit of area. 1*mu*＝0.066,7 hectares). The freshwater fish with great economic values are grass carp, silver carp, bighead carp, cyprinoid, crucian carp, gurnard, black fish, eel, mandarin fish, Bachymystax lenok and so on. In addition, there are many freshwater shrimps and freshwater crabs.

Hebei is located in the juncture area between the warm temperate zone and the temperate zone. As one of the provinces rich in plant resources in China, Hebei has a wide variety of vegetation. Based on the preliminary statistics of Hebei, there are altogether 156 families and more than 3,000 species of vegetation. The main crops cultivated in Hebei include food crops, such as wheat, maize, millet, rice, sorghum, beans,

Brown Eared Pheasant
褐马鸡

etc., and cash crops, such as cotton, oil plants and bast fibre plants, etc. There are more than 500 species of woody plants, including more than 100 species of timber trees. Among them, some species are famous at home and abroad, such as Populus gansuensis, Toona sinensis (A. Juss.) Roem, and Quercus variabilis Bl., etc. Some species are of high economic value, such as Picea asperata Mast., Pinus tabuliformis Carr., Platycladus orientalis(L.)Francoptmxjjkmsc, Larix principis-rupprechtii Mayr, Ulmus pumila L., linden, Styphnolobium japonicum(L.) Schott, Pteroceltis tatarinowii Maxim., and Mallotus (Lam.) paniculatus Müll. Arg., and Betula, etc., and some special economic tree species are also distributed in Hebei, such as Toxicodendron

vernicifluum (Stokes) F. A. Barkl., Eucommia ulmoides, Paulownia and Pistacia chinensis, etc. There are more than 100 kinds of fruit trees in the province, and the dried fruits produced here are chestnuts, walnuts, Chinese prickly ashes, etc. The chestnut production in Hebei accounts for 1/4 of the total production in China, ranking first in the country. And the fresh fruits produced in Hebei mainly are pears, apples, hawthorn fruits, apricots, peaches, grapes, persimmons, plums and pomegranates, etc., among which the output of pears ranks first in China.

Many fruits in Hebei are famous and sell well both at home and abroad, such as Zhaoxian snowflake pears, Shenzhou peaches, Xuanhua grapes, Changli apples, Cangzhou golden-silk jujubes, Fuping big jujubes, Zanhuang big jujubes, and Qianxi chestnuts, etc. Shrubs are widely distributed in Hebei, including some shrubs that produce wild fruits and some shrubs that are of medicinal value. Hebei has many kinds of herbaceous plants, with more than 300 kinds in the Bashang Plateau alone, including many kinds of fine forage grasses, such as Leymus chinensis, Bromus inermis, Agropyron cristatum, Medicago sativa and Vicia amoena Fisch. ex DC. More than 800 kinds of plants in Hebei have been used for medical treatment. The main medicinal plants include the well-known Puerarialobata, Glycyrrhiza uralensis, Ephedra sinica, Rheum palmatum L., Codonopsis pilosula, Lycium chinense, Ziziphus jujuba, Bupleurum chinense, Saposhnikovia divaricata, Rhizoma anemarrhenae, Angelica dahurica, Polygala tenuifolia, Platycodon grandiflorus, Mentha canadensis and Scutellaria baicalensis, etc.

Chapter 4
The Transport Network in Hebei

—An Outlet Toward the East, a Connecting Point Toward the West, and an Integral Part of Beijing-Tianjin-Hebei Transport Integration

Hebei is located in the eastern part of China, along the Pacific coast. Topographically, in China's three-step terrain structure, Hebei is on the third step. With many good harbors, it is located in a favorable geographical location as "an outlet toward the east and a connecting point toward the west", forming the interactive pattern between the coast and the inland of China as well as within Hebei and between Hebei and other provinces, which enables it to make better use of both international and domestic markets and resources.

Caofeidian Port of Tangshan
曹妃甸港

As "an outlet toward the east", Hebei can take advantage of its eastern ports and coastal economic logistics system to provide a convenient access to the sea for North China and northwest provinces. As "a connecting point toward the west", Hebei can strengthen economic and trade cooperation with Beijing, Tianjin and other provinces, such as Shanxi, Shaanxi, and Inner Mongolia, etc., and connect with the economic areas on the north and west sides of the Great Wall, so as to achieve complementary advantages. Encircling Beijing and Tianjin and embracing the Bohai Sea, Hebei is located in a favorable geographical location. As "an outlet toward the east", Hebei can make full use of its 487 km coastline to develop its port industrial zones like Shanghai, building a prosperous coastal economic belt and integrating into the economic zone along the Bohai Sea. As "a connecting point toward the west", Hebei can establish connections with the economic areas on the north and west sides of the Great Wall including more than a dozen cities such as Hohhot, Datong, Yulin, Lanzhou, extend industries toward the inland, and continuously provide primary products and energy for the manufacturing industries in the economic zone along the Bohai Sea.

Hebei is the transport hub connecting the capital Beijing with all the other parts of China. All the main railways and highways leading from Beijing to other places must pass through Hebei to radiate outwards. Hebei is also the place that must be passed for Beijing to communicate and contact with important economic regions, such as Northwest China, North China, Northeast China, South China and East China so as to exchange goods and resources, so it takes a very important strategic position in transportation.

In 2015, *The Guidelines for Coordinated Development of the Beijing-Tianjin-Hebei Region* was approved by the the Politburo of the Central Committee of the CPC. According to the guidelines, promoting the coordinated development of the Beijing-Tianjin-Hebei region is a major national strategy, the core of which is to orderly move non-capital functions out of Beijing, and the breakthroughs should be made firstly in some key areas, such as the Beijing-Tianjin-Hebei transport integration, the ecological conservation, the environmental protection, and the industrial upgrading and relocation.

The Beijing-Tianjin-Hebei transport integration has been taken as the priority area in promoting the coordinated development to accelerate the construction of a fast, convenient, efficient, safe, interconnected and comprehensive transport network with large capacity and low cost. By the end of 2021, the railroad mileage in Hebei had reached 8,050 km, ranking second in China; its highway mileage had reached 209,500 km, including 8,087 km of expressway, ranking fourth in China; its annual design traffic-capacity had reached 1.13 billion tons, ranking third in China; the total number of its airports had grown to 16 with 2 newly-built general airports. The comprehensive transport routes of "four vertical, four horizontal and one loop routes" had basically taken shape in the Beijing-Tianjin-Hebei region. Such a pattern of transport network has been continuously optimized.

The external main road network in Xiong'an New Area has been fully built up. In 2021, the transport system endeavored to promote the construction of the main road network around Xiong'an New Area. The Jingxiong Expressway, the new line of the Rongwu Expressway, the first phase of Jingde Expressway, the Rongyi Expressway, and the Anda Expressway have been completed and put into use, opening up the "four vertical and three horizontal" transport arteries of Xiong'an New Area.

Xiong'an Railway Station
雄安站

The plan of "Beijing-Tianjin-Hebei on rails" will create a new pattern of regional transport. Many railways, including Beijing-Tianjin Intercity Extension Railway, Beijing-Zhangjiakou High-speed Railway, Beijing-Xiong'an Intercity Railway, and Beijing-Chengde section of Beijing-Harbin High-speed Railway, etc., have been completed and opened to traffic. The construction of sub-center station hubs, Fengtai railway station, Chaoyang railway station, and the supporting traffic hubs have been accelerated. All these efforts are to accelerate the construction of an integrated transport network in the Beijing-Tianjin-Hebei region, through which you can get to another neighboring city by train within 1.5 hours, and the "one-hour commuting circle" has been formed among Beijing, Xiong'an, Tianjin and Baoding.

Up to now, 23 railways have been build to connect Hebei with Beijing and Tianjin, so the main framework of "Beijing-Tianjin-Hebei on rails" has basically taken shape. With the completion and commissioning of many railways, such as Beijing-Zhangjiakou High-speed Railway, Tianjin-Qinhuangdao High-speed Railway, Beijing-Harbin High-speed Railway, Beijing-Xiong'an Intercity Railway and Tianjin-Baoding Intercity Railway, all cities in Hebei have been covered by the high-speed railway network. As to highways, Hebei has opened and widened 34 "docking roads" connecting with Beijing and Tianjin, with a total mileage of 2,089 kilometers. The number of arterial highways connecting Hebei with Beijing and Tianjin has reached 47, with 74 joining intersections. In terms of expressways, some key projects, such as the Capital Ring Expressway and Taihang Mountain Expressway, have been completed and opened to traffic. The expressway mileage in Hebei has reached 8,087 kilometers, and all counties in Hebei have been covered by the expressway network.

The large ports along the coast of Hebei, such as Tangshan Port, Qinhuangdao Port and Huanghua Port, are the important accesses to the sea for North China (including Beijing) and Northwest China. The number of productive berths in the coastal ports of Hebei has reached 242, with a design traffic-capacity of 1.13 billion tons and an annual throughput exceeding 1.2 billion tons. These ports have established trade relations with more than 400 ports of other countries all over the world. Caofeidian Port of Tangshan, one of the natural deep-water harbors, owns the harbour

Taihang Mountain Expressway in Shexian County, Handan City

邯郸涉县 太行山高速

and natural waterway in Bohai Sea that do not need to be excavated. It is a port with multiple berths and with the largest individual engineering quantity in China, which is capable of docking 300,000-ton vessels. The bulk cargo throughput of Qinhuangdao Port ranks first among all the bulk cargo ports in the world. As the most convenient and economical access to the sea in the central and the southern area of Hebei, Huanghua Port is accelerating its construction of multifunctional comprehensive port area. In terms of airports, the layout of the Beijing-Tianjin-Hebei airport cluster has been perfected at an accelerated pace. The number of airports in Hebei has reached 16, and the layout system of "one hub with multiple branches and points" has taken its initial shape.

By now, a safe, convenient, efficient, green and economic comprehensive transport system has been basically established, and the development of the transport integration in this region has accelerated the circulation and turnover of various production factors in the region, which has a significant effect on the economic development and industrial structure optimization of the Beijing-Tianjin-Hebei region.

Chapter 5
The Cultural Characteristics of Hebei

—Yan-Zhao Culture Overlapped with the Culture of the Capital and Its Environs

Psychologist Carl Gustav Jung (1875—1961) once put forward the concept of "collective unconsciousness". It means that a race or group can form an unconscious cultural structure through thousands of years of accumulation and precipitation under different cultural environments, and such a structure invisibly provides the advanced modes of thinking and behavior. To better understand the cultural characteristics of Hebei, we need to travel through time and space, listening to the distant echoes from history, so as to figure out how the "collective unconsciousness" in the land of Yan-Zhao has come into being.

Hebei is one of the important birthplaces of Chinese civilization. During the Pre-Qin Period, Yan culture, Zhao culture and Zhongshan culture had emerged on this land. Since the

Wearing the Hu Attire and Shooting from Horseback
胡服骑射

establishment of the capitals of the Jin and Yuan Dynasties, the unique culture of the capital and its environs have been formed in Hebei. The culture of Yan-Zhao and the culture of the capital and its environs overlapped with each other, which has formed the profound cultural heritage and the unique cultural characteristics of the modern Hebei.

Hebei was called "Yan-Zhao" during the Spring and Autumn Period and the Warring States Period. It is not only a geographical term. In fact, the culture of Yan-Zhao of those periods has long shaped the culture of Hebei and the character of its people, finally formed the collective unconsciousness of this area, and has been influencing them to this day. So Yan-Zhao culture refers to the particular culture system, which has been formed based on the relationship between man and nature and the relationship between man and man in the long history of Hebei. In other words, Yan-Zhao culture is a general term of the material culture, the institutional culture, the ideology, and the lifestyle formed in Hebei region. As the most prominent culture in Hebei, Yan-Zhao culture includes the following aspects.

Firstly, the gallant and chivalrous character, the passionate and tragic heroism, the revolutionary and enterprising spirit, and the inner drive of endless self-improvement.

Geographically, Hebei is roughly bounded by the Yanshan Mountains, the Taihang Mountains, the Yellow River and the Bohai Sea. According to historical records, Hebei had always been in a state of "bordering the non-Han barbarians in the north and west, and often being invaded". Located at the forefront of the dividing line between the agricultural and nomadic civilizations, Hebei often faced the conflicts and wars between them, which had run through the whole process of its history. Such conflicts and wars can be traced back to as early as the Battle of Banquan between Yandi and Huangdi (two mythical emperors), and continued until the Manchu entered the Central Plains in the Qing Dynasty. As a political symbol that the emperor's reign had covered the whole China, Emperor Kangxi built Chengde Imperial Summer Resort and Mulan Paddock in Chengde, thus the conflicts of civilizations were replaced by the integration of civilizations.

In the Spring and Autumn Period and the Warring States Period, the territory of Hebei was mainly occupied by the two states of Yan and Zhao. In addition, in this land, there was a mysterious state of Zhongshan, which is said to be a kingdom established by the White Di tribes. It was destroyed twice and then restored twice, and was eventually destroyed by the state of Zhao during the reign of King Wuling of Zhao and then incorporated into the territory of Zhao. The differences between Yan and Zhao are quite obvious. The history of Yan started much earlier than that of Zhao. When Zhao was founded by dividing Jin together with Han and Wei, Yan had already existed for at least 600 years. However, Yan was almost unknown throughout the Western Zhou Dynasty and the Spring and Autumn Period, always in a cramped, constrained and weak situation, thus forming what later generations called the "Bitter Cold Culture". In the middle and late Warring States Period, Yan began to rise. During the reign of King Zhao of Yan, its national strength increased greatly after 28 years' accumulation by taking the strategy of keeping a low profile and hiding its capacities. He appointed Yue Yi as the general and completely defeated Qi with the help of the troops of the other five states, which shocked all the states and forced them to give a new appraisal of Yan. But after the death of King Zhao of Yan, Yan quickly declined. After the Battle of Changping between Qin and Zhao, and when the army of Qin approached the Yishui River, Yan was in deadly danger. In order to save the state, Prince Dan planned to kill the king of Qin, and he found an assassinator named Jing Ke. The famous poem depicts the scene that Jing Ke bade his farewell by the Yishui River:

> Hsiao-hsiao soughs the wind, oh-
> Cold the waters of the Yi.
> The knight who leaves you now, oh-
> You shall nevermore see. [*Translated by James I. Crump Jr. (1970—　)*]

The above verse is not only an elegy for the state of Yan, but also a demonstration of the heroic spirit of the Yan people.

After the collapse of Jin, Zhao, as one of the three powers (Han, Zhao and Wei) that defeated and divided Jin up, was established. Then its political center was moved from Jinyang (today's Taiyuan, Shanxi) to Handan (today's Handan, Hebei). It took a relatively long period of time for Zhao to take Hebei instead of Shanxi as its main body. Zhao was located in the region exposed to enemy attacks on all sides and surrounded all by strong neighboring states. So it faced not only the annexation wars between the regional states but also the harassment from the nomads. Besides, the mysterious Zhongshan State even once embedded itself deep into the hinterland of Zhao. During the reign of King Wuling of Zhao, he carried out a vigorous reform consisting of "Wearing the Hu Attire

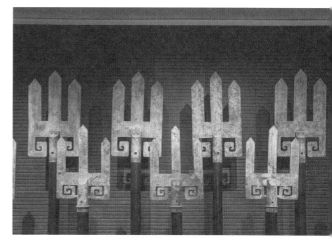

Zhongshan Guo *shan*-shaped ritual vessel
战国中山国 山字型礼器

and Shooting from Horseback", in order to remove the threat to the whole state. In the era with strict boundaries between Huaxia culture and other neighbouring cultures, you can imagine how courageous and decisive he must be when he took the initiative to learn from the nomads. This reform not only changed the fate of Zhao, but also opened a window for the integration of different cultures while they fought against each other on the land of Yan-Zhao. By reforms, King Wuling of Zhao destroyed the state of Zhongshan, and finally eliminated the sting in his heart. In the process of its rapid rise, Zhao always took openness, inclusiveness, enterprising spirit and martial spirit as its national spirit, thus forming its particular heroic temperament. The cultural character differences between Yan and Zhao were integrated and gradually formed an entity through the two periods of the First Emperor of Qin's territorial unification and Emperor Wu of Western Han's ideological unification. Later it was identified as the historical complex of "the passionate and tragic heroism", which has become a significant symbol of Yan-Zhao culture and a unique spiritual character of Hebei people.

Secondly, emphasizing sage-warrior temperament, pursuing harmony and cooperation, and placing collective interests above personal interests.

The peculiarity of the land of Yan-Zhao is that the chivalrous men brought up here were not simple-minded warriors. They were not just all brawn and no brains as we may think. They were both gentle and brave, mastering both the pen and the sword. This combined character is exactly one of the cultural genes of Yan-Zhao people, which makes this land different from other places. At the end of the Warring States Period, Xunzi, a native of Zhao, was born here. He was a maverick in the formation process of Confucianism. While Confucius stressed the importance of "obeying the mandate of heaven", Xunzi unprecedentedly declared that man's will, not heaven, decides. While Mencius's theory of original goodness of human nature was popular, Xunzi boldly advocated the theory of original evil of human nature... His thoughts were quite different from the Confucian moral idealism of his time. He reconstructed a conceptual system of social criticism, and therefore was called "the ranger of Confucianism" by later generations. Xunzi is a great scholar nurtured by Yan-Zhao chivalrous culture. In turn, his thoughts have also nurtured Yan-Zhao culture for more than 2,000 years. The famous Confucian scholars of later generations in Yan-Zhao region, such as Shao Yong, Sun Qifeng and Yan Yuan, mostly inherited the chivalrous character of Xunzi in their spirit and temperament. They didn't attach themselves to emperors, nor readily agreed with other scholars, nor pandered to the taste of the vulgar people. They just calmly and bravely declared and practiced their own unique thoughts and codes of conduct. After Xunzi, Confucianism has been inherited and never interrupted in this region. Even during the Period of Wei, Jin, and Southern and Northern Dynasties when metaphysics and Buddhism prevailed while Confucianism was very weak all over the country, Confucianism still flourished in this region. According to historical records, the scholars in Yan-Zhao region at that time still engaged themselves in the study of Confucian classics rather than Buddhism and Taoism. Yan Zhitui, who had long lived in this region, admonished his descendants in his work *Family Instructions of Master Yan* not to give up reading the books of sages. Although during the chaotic Southern and Northern Dynasties, when the north of China was ruled by other ethnic groups, the academic tradition had been preserved in this region through the aristocratic families, and had later influenced the foreign rulers and assimilated them gradually. In the dynasties after Emperor Wudi of the Western Han Dynasty, the living space of chivalrous men was basically strangled. However, this chivalrous spirit gradually merged and became a part of the spirit of scholars of this region, thus forming the unique sage-warrior temperament. Such a temperament of Yan-Zhao region can be traced back to Lin Xiangru, the famous prime minister of Zhao in the Warring States Period. In some historical stories, such as "returning the Jade intact to the state of Zhao" and "meeting at Mianchi to form the alliance between Qin and Zhao", facing the powerful rival of Qin, Lin Xiangru unexpectedly broke the conventional diplomatic rules and twice threatened the king of Qin to kill himself on the spot to show his determination of fighting against the humiliation from Qin. He would like to die and break the jade rather than surrender under the pressure, and to splash his own blood on the body of the king of Qin, who sat just close enough to him (within five steps) rather than let Zhao be humiliated by Qin. However, when his colleague Lian Po, the general of Zhao, rudely humiliated him, Lin Xiangru could endure the humiliation

Sculpture of the Fight against Japanese Aggressors on the Great Wall
长城抗战雕塑

for the sake of the state interests. A great man should know when to yield and when not just like what Lin Xiangru once did. It is a noble spirit to put collective interests above individual interests and consciously pursue harmony and cooperation under the condition of acknowledging the differences between each other, which has not only exerted profound influence on the people of Yan-Zhao, but has also inspired Chinese people generation after generation.

Thirdly, the qualities of being industrious, honest, devoted, and courteous.

The cultural character of Yan-Zhao region has been gradually accumulated and formed in the long history, but it is not static. Since the Jin and Yuan Dynasties, Beijing, which is an inseparable part of Yan-Zhao region, became the capitals of the several unified dynasties thereafter, so the capital culture began to permeate into Yan-Zhao culture. Influenced by the capital culture, the culture of Hebei had a new development in the integration of the capital culture and the former Yan-Zhao culture. Many places in Hebei are the embodiment of the capital culture, such as Chengde Imperial Summer Resort, Eastern Royal Tombs of the Qing Dynasty in Zunhua City and Western Royal Tombs of the Qing Dynasty in Yixian County (a county in Baoding, Hebei). The region of ancient Yan-Zhao culture surrounding Beijing was basically the core area of the environs of the capitals in the Yuan, Ming and Qing Dynasties. In the Qing Dynasty, this region was called Zhili Province, which literally means "directly ruled (province)". Its status was quite unique in the entire empire. However, this uniqueness didn't not mean that more resources or special support could be obtained from the central government, but rather, it meant dedication, sacrifice and suffer. When Chang'an, Luoyang and Kaifeng were the capitals of the previous dynasties, Yan-Zhao region was at the forefront of the conflicts between agricultural and nomadic civilizations. As a strategically important area, it was difficult for the people here to live a peaceful life. They were under much more burdens and stress than people elsewhere. When Beijing became the capital of the empire, Yan-Zhao region became a place strictly controlled by the imperial forces. It had to assume the functions of serving the capital city, relieving the natural disasters of the capital, and bearing the impact of political struggles. Under the strict constraints of the imperial power, the people here gradually began to restrain their heroic and chivalrous character, and became silent. Therefore, the character of tolerance and loyalty gradually prevailed, and became the prominent cultural character of Zhili people for this period of time. Actually, for the people of Hebei, the character of tolerance and loyalty is just like a dominant gene as shown in the surface, while their righteous and chivalrous character is like a recessive gene hidden deep inside. Only when major social crises happen, will the hidden character of Hebei people be revealed, demonstrating the fighting spirit inherited from Yan-Zhao culture. That is why the people of Hebei are able to leave indelible marks in Chinese history with their courage and strength in every turbulent period, even after being strictly constrained hundreds of years right under the emperors' nose.

In the Ming Dynasty, when treacherous officials appeared at the court, there came Yang Jisheng, a "tough guy" from Hebei, who bravely stood up against those evil political forces; after the fall of the Ming Dynasty, Sun Qifeng, a legendary and righteous historical figure and a Neo-Confucianist from Hebei, boldly and repeatedly refused to yield to the powerful; During the Hundred Days Reform period of the Qing Dynasty, the heroic deeds of Wang Zhengyi, also known as "big sword Wang Wu" from Hebei, were well known in China; when the Chinese people were exploring a new path in the new era, a young man named Li Dazhao stood up from Hebei, who was one of the founders of the Communist Party of China and played an important role in the Communist movement; when China was invaded by the Japanese, many heroic deeds against Japanese invaders happened in Hebei, such as the battle in and around Xifengkou Great Wall Pass, and the five heroes of Langya Mountain... The people here showed an indomitable spirit when facing enemies, and countless heroes stood up one by one to fight against the invaders. The spirit of "passionate and tragic heroism" often reappeared in the land of Yan-Zhao in times of crisis. After more than 2,000 years of time, you may think such a unique sage-warrior spirit has become the fossil of history. However, it has turned into a chivalrous spirit deeply hidden in the hearts of Hebei people: a collective unconscious that can break out at any time when facing the threat of external forces.

The history of Hebei can be regarded as a microcosm of Chinese history. Since ancient times, every step of the history of Chinese civilization has left traces on this land. In traditional Chinese thought, agricultural and nomadic civilizations were always in a state of confrontation, as if there were natural barriers between them. But in fact, there is no clear dividing line between any two things, and even the Great Wall is not a clear dividing line in the sense of civilization. Inside and outside the Great Wall, the fusion and conflict of the two civilizations occurred from time to time. In history, Hebei had wavered on this line, and had been the wrestling field of the two civilizations, functioning as a "stomach" where the two civilizations were mixed and digested. Today, there is still a flavor of nomadic civilization in northern Hebei, such as in some areas of Chengde and Zhangjiakou. Bashang Grassland, Mulan Paddock and Chengde Imperial Summer Resort, all indicate the integration of these two civilizations in history. The central and southern parts of Hebei are the most typical embodiment of the agricultural civilization in the Central Plains. Handan is a rare city that has kept its name for more than 3,000 years, which could be regarded as a metaphor for cultural stability. Since modern times, with the rise of marine civilization, Hebei has been standing at the forefront of accepting and absorbing the influence of foreign civilizations. In the eastern part of Hebei, the cities such as Qinhuangdao, Tangshan and Cangzhou are all located along the Bohai Sea, where the First Emperor of Qin once carried on his inspection tour, and Cao Cao once whipped his steed galloping on this land and wrote his heroic poems. Today, it has become a place where China' modern industry is rising and where the sea shipping is flourishing. Here ancient and modern spirits often overlap, and history and reality are often intertwined at some moments.

In light of historical experience, we can see that the people in Hebei would hide their light under a bushel in peace times. Even in the face of difficulties and troubles, they would restrain themselves and continue their lives in silence. However, in times of crisis, they would definitely resort to their "passionate and heroic heroism" formed in history, stand out boldly and shock the whole world with their sage-warrior spirit. This is the cultural characteristics and the inner spirit of Hebei people.

 **Exercises**

Ⅰ. Comprehension

（1）What are the four geographical boundaries of China? Are there any similarities between them?

（2）Please talk about the landforms in Hebei. Why is Hebei called the "miniature of China's geography"?

（3）What is Hebei called for short? How did the name come from?

（4）How does the railway mileage of Hebei rank in China? And how about its highway mileage? How many ports are there in Hebei?

Ⅱ. Translation

1. Term Translation

（1）京畿重地

（2）东出西联

（3）慷慨悲歌

（4）京津冀协同发展

2. Passage Translation

河北虽为畿辅重地，又负阴抱阳、背山面水，却因为形状破碎、整体经济不振等原因，难以给人们留下一个完整而深刻的印象。放眼河北省内，在"环首都""环渤海"的"两环"战略一路高歌猛进的大背景下，位于内陆腹地的冀中南地区则显得尤其落寞。殊不知该地却有一条盛产古都的大走廊，在历史的尘封中默默诉说着曾经的辉煌。

Part Two

Wonders of Nature: The Beauty of Mountains and Rivers

Located in the boundary zone between coastal and inland areas, Hebei is the only province in China to contain all kinds of landforms including plateaus, plains, lakes, mountains, hills, basins and shorelines. Distinctive landforms and landscape features endow the land with uniqueness: Beidaihe's golden sands and blue waves add colors to the planet; Zhangshiyan's long red cliffs show magnificent momentum; Kongshan Baiyun Cave, which comprises five components, fully presents the beauty of nature. The diverse landforms of Hebei form different types of climates, providing suitable habitats for all kinds of plants and animals. Yesanpo, Liaoheyuan, Bashang Grassland and Mount Wuling are all excellent scenic spots to appreciate the abundant and precious animal and plant resources of Hebei while climbing the mountains and enjoying the scenery.

Baiyangdian Fishing Song
白洋淀渔歌

Lead-in Questions

(1) Before reading this part, please give an example of the natural scenery in Hebei that you are familiar with.

(2) Based on Chapter I "The Geographical Features of Hebei" in Part One, please discuss with your partner why Hebei has these natural wonders.

(3) Along the east foot of the Taihang Mountains, from south to north, please list examples of the unique scenery of Hebei.

(4) Is Hebei a coastal province? Which cities in Hebei are coastal cities?

Chapter 6

Beidaihe

—A Popular Resort to Embrace Cool and Comfortable Summer with Blue Sea and Golden Beach

The Seaside-Beidaihe[1]

By Mao Zedong (Summer, 1954)

On northern land a heavy rain is pouring,

Sky-high white waves are roaring.

Off Emperor's Isle the fishing boats outgoing

All lost to sight in the wide, wide sea foaming,

Who knows where they are roaming?

Over a thousand years ago by the seaside,

Whipping his steed, Wu of Wei[2] *took a ride.*

Verses on his eastern trip to Mount Stone still remain.

The autumn wind is blowing now as bleak as then,

But changed is the world of men.

Beidaihe is the most renowned natural seaside resort in northern China, with a long and winding coastline, smooth beaches, golden soft sand and clear shallow water. In recent years, archaeologists discovered and excavated a group of large architectural complex site in the south

---

[1] Beidaihe is a famous seaside resort not far from Qinhuangdao or Emperor of Qin's Isle, an ice-free port in the northern land.

[2] King Wu or the Martial King of Wei (155—220) was one of the three kings who tried to unify the empire in the period of Three Kingdoms. In 207 he came on a horse to the Rocky Hill or Mount Stone (in today's Changli County of Qinghuangdao).

(The above contents are all extracted from, *Selected Poems of Mao Zedong* (The 2020 Edition) translated by Xu Yuanchong and published by China Publishing Group Corporation, China Translation & Publishing House).

Beidaihe Wetland Park
北戴河湿地公园

of Hengshan Mountain in Beidaihe. According to research and deduction, the underground finding proves to be the residence of Qin Shi Huang (the founder of the Qin Dynasty) during his eastern tour, which has been listed as one of the national key protected cultural relic units by the State Council. A block of Western-style villas and Chinese-style pavilions are seated there nowadays, reaching a total of more than 3,000 buildings with recently-built and well-equipped hotels and inns counted in. Every year, the site attracts millions of domestic tourists and groups of foreign guests and tourists from nearly 100 countries and regions.

Beidaihe is located 15 kilometers southwest of Qinhuangdao City, with Lianfeng Mountain standing gracefully on its north and the waves of a wide sea lapping its south coastline. The seaside resort area enjoys picturesque scenery and pleasant climate. Fresh air in spring, warm wind in winter, clear sky and tranquility in autumn, and cool weather in summer—even in the sixth and seventh month of the lunar calendar, the hottest days of summer, the average temperature is only 23 ℃—compose the loveliness of Beidaihe. The resort stretches about 13 kilometers from east to west, from Geziwo Park (Dove Nest Park) and Yingjiao Pavilion to Daihekou (the Daihe River estuary). And it is about 2 kilometers in width, so the coastal zone comes in an elongated shape. The beach is covered with soft sand and the tide is gentle, making the area a good choice for sea bathing. Majestic mountains, sunny beaches, quiet villas, pretty gardens, together decorate the seaside colorful and splendid. In midsummer, tourists to Beidaihe always revel in the charming scenery—watching the sunrise in the morning, bathing in the sea at noon, watching the tides in the evening, walking on the beach with the bright moon shining high overhead, and enjoying the whistling of the wind in the pines and the rush of the sea. Everyone visiting here will feel completely relaxed. As a famous destination in China and a renowned summer resort and health resort at home and abroad, Beidaihe has been listed as a national key scenic area.

Favorite attractions of Beidaihe include Lianfeng Mountain, Biluo Tower Bar Park, Geziwo Park, Tiger Stone Marine Park, Guai Lou Park, etc., all with different characteristics and charms. Mountains here are painted exceptionally green while the sea looks like an enormous pool of wonder in azure blue. The sun rises and sets; the tides ebb and flow; the sky clouds down and clears up…. The scenery changes even within a single day but keeps spectacular and stunning.

Lianfeng Mountain Park, also known as Lianpeng Mountain Park, lies at the west of Beidaihe Scenic Area with a distance of 5 kilometers from east to west. First built in 1919, it is the largest forest park of this area famous for the joy of walking in the mountains and exploring the winding paths. Lianfeng Mountain literally means "connected peaks", because the pine-covered three peaks, namely East Peak, Middle Peak, and West Peak vertically arranged from south to north, are connected with each other. The park is also called Lianpeng Mountain Park (Lotus Pod Mountain Park) because of the fact that the mountain looks like a lotus pod from afar. Standing at an altitude of 153 meters, the East Peak is the highest among all the three peaks, offering a sea-view pavilion where tourists can appreciate the overall fantastic scenery of the park. Beautiful and mighty mountains, dense forests, deep valleys, strange stones and caves, every step unfolds the ever-changing but timeless beauty of nature. Various styles of buildings and villas hide in the large stretches of pine forests, adding exquisite taste to the unspoiled land. In the 1990s, the ruins of the Han Dynasty were discovered on the top of the Middle Lianfeng Mountain and were named "Hanwu Platform". It is believed Emperor Wudi of the Han Dynasty who yearned for immortality had built it to worship gods, so the mystery of this old land is still to be unveiled gradually. Picturesque and tranquil view of the decorated mountains and the sea, as well as the lush plants and colorful flowers, have made here attractive to countless visitors from ancient times to modern times.

Biluo Tower Bar Park is situated at Xiaodongshan, the eastern end of Beidaihe, and surrounded by sea on three sides. The Biluo Tower, the main building of the park, is the only conch-shaped spiral tower in the world,

Biluo Tower Bar Park
碧螺塔公园

providing visitors with the grand and joyous sea scenery as the highest building of the coastal area. Reefs standing around the Biluo Tower create a cradle for plankton, and the park is appointed as a sea fishing base for the rich resources of fish, crabs, shellfish and other marine biological resources. Deng Xiaoping, one of the greatest men in China, came here for recreational fishing several times. In memory of him, a monument of "Deng Xiaoping Fishing Spot" was put up, and the "Biluo Tower Sea Fishing Base" was established in 2003, with the "Beidaihe Sea Fishing Festival" held from September to October every year. Over 50 vessels of all sizes and a variety of fishing gear and nets are prepared for inshore fishing, offshore fishing and deep-sea fishing.

Located at the easternmost terminus of Beidaihe, Geziwo Park covers an area of more than 300 mu and is also regarded as the best sunrise spot. The destination got the name for its geographic formation: on the cliff facing the sea formed by the fracture, stands the 20-meter-high Yingjiao Stone with the shape of an eagle; flocks of pigeons used to gather or nest in the cracks of the stone, hence the name "Geziwo" (which means "Dove Nest" in English) is given. Every summer morning, tens of thousands of tourists gather here to enjoy the scenery of "red sun shining on the sea". Taking a walk along the 182-meter-long waterfront corridor, feeling the gentle sea breezes, sitting quietly under the cherry trees beside the blue water, and watching the white birds flying high above, visitors enjoy such fun-filled holiday, relaxing and refreshing.

Tiger Stone Marine Park, located in the center of Beidaihe, has a total area of 33,000 square meters. Different types of reefs scatter in the park, looking like a group of tigers. The broad beach and wide sea, taking the advantage of the gentle slope under the clear water, has become the bathing beach with the largest number of tourists in summer. Also, integrating elements of leisure and amusement, the park is equipped with parasailing equipment, windsurfing boards, surfboards, children's "paradise", etc., making it a comparatively big seaside comprehensive park in China at present. To the west of the park, there is a small dock, which was constructed in 1957 with the special approval of Zhu De, one of the major founders of the People's Republic of China, where tourists can dock yachts and boats and go fishing and sightseeing. To the west of

the dock, there stands "Wanggui Pavilion" ("Turtle-watching Pavilion"), small but exquisitely built.

　　Beidaihe is also known as a birding haven. According to relevant records, there are 1,186 species of birds in China, and 405 species from 61 families and 20 orders in Beidaihe alone. Among them, 68 species are under national key protection, many of which are world-famous rare birds. Early in the 20th century, ornithologists from the United States, Germany and other countries came to investigate bird resources and wrote monographs. In recent years, batches of bird researchers and bird lovers from Britain, the United States, Japan, Denmark, Belgium, Australia and other countries have paid visits to conduct academic research and bird-watching activities. Experts consider Beidaihe one of the best bases for bird watching and bird research.

Chapter 7
Mount Wuling

—A Sacred Buddhist Cultural Mountain, A Summer Resort of Deep Enchantment

Mount Wuling, located in Xinglong County, is the main peak of the Yanshan Mountains. The well-protected virgin forests make the mountain live up to its reputation of "Gene Bank of Species in North China".

In his *Records of Mountains and Rivers in Changping*, Gu Yanwu, an outstanding philosopher in the late Ming and early Qing dynasties, described Mount Wuling as "a high and steep mountain enveloped in clouds and mist, displaying the same beauty all year round". This may be the reason why Wuling Mountain got its name, because "wu" means "misty", and "ling" means "soul" or "soul-related" in Chinese.

Mount Wuling
雾灵山

Early in the Song Dynasty, Mount Wuling had become a famous religious mountain. A large number of temples were constructed here, with "over 10,000 Buddhist monks and nuns". Gu Yanwu's *Records of Mountains and Rivers in Changping* documented Buddhist ceremonies in the Yuan Dynasty—"Jayaatu Khan, Emperor Wenzong (1304—1332) of the Yuan Dynasty, once sent monks in the western regions to conduct Buddhist activities in Mount Wuling for a month." The sites of Hongmei Temple, Zhong Guyuan, and Yunfeng Temple, which used to be called the Lower, Middle and Upper Houses, exist to this day. It is said that in the past "there were 3,600 famous monks and countless nameless monks" in Hongmei Temple, proving its reputation as the sacred mountain of Buddhism. During the reign of Emperor Hongwu of the Ming Dynasty (1368—1398), Liu Ji (his courtesy name is Bowen), an assistant minister of justice, paid a visit to Caojialu, an important border town. On his way, he climbed Mount Wuling. Halfway up the mountain, tired and hot, he rested beside a boulder; suddenly he felt a cool breeze sweeping his fatigue away, thus writing down six Chinese characters "雾灵山清凉界", which means "Wuling Mountain, a cool world" to mark this refreshing moment. Two hundred years later, in the eighth year of the reign of Emperor Chongzhen of the Ming Dynasty (1635), these words written down by Liu Ji were engraved on this boulder as a memorial, which has become a unique stone monument located to the east of Beijing, known as the "Dazi Stone" ("Big Character Stone"). On the stone, each character is about 4 square meters in size, bold and free, vigorous and powerful. In the second year of the reign of Emperor Shunzhi of the Qing Dynasty (1645), Mount Wuling was designated as the "forbidden land", and was banned for 270 years, because according to Chinese fengshui, this mountain range runs like a dragon protecting the southern Eastern Royal Tombs of the Qing Dynasty. Emperor Kangxi[1] of the Qing Dynasty, once wrote in his poem *Starting from Gubeikou in the Morning, and Looking at Wuling Mountain from a Distance*: "Blowing liuchui (an ancient musical instrument) we set out in the early morning and march to the border, with battle flags flying in the wind. The moon still hangs on the distant peak,

---

[1] Kangxi: with posthumous title, Shengzu, which literally means "ancestor of sage".

and clouds float around the ancient trees. There are few traces of human beings in this remote area, and only the pounding of horses' hooves echo among the mountains. For sightseeing, the scenery of summer is the best, when the flowers and grass in the valley are fragrant." Under the long years' ban of the Qing Dynasty, Mount Wuling created ideal conditions for the growth of forest and the reproduction of wild animals, forming such magnificent landscape of "thick forests stretch as far as the eye could see, and enormous mighty trees block the sun; numerous wild animals chase each other in the woods, and springs and streams bubble up out of the rocks".

After the founding of the People's Republic of China, a special organization was set up to protect this precious green land. The beauty and charm of Mount Wuling is thereby preserved thanks to the careful and effective management.

In 1988 the Mount Wuling National Nature Reserve was approved by the State Council as the first national nature reserve in Hebei Province. Covering 15,000 hectares, the reserve is established to protect "the temperate forest ecosystem" and "the north limit of the distribution of

Daurian Redstart in Mount Wuling
雾灵山的北红尾鸲

macaque". As an area with "the temperate forest ecosystem", Mount Wuling is located at the intersection of the three floristic regions of Mongolia, Northeast China and North China. Owing to the vast variety of plant components and the correspondingly complex and diverse ecosystem, the mountain has become a reserve of temperate biodiversity and a treasure house of biological resources. As "the north limit of the distribution of macaque", Mount Wuling serves as an indication in the world that there are no wild primates living to its north. The mountain is also the north-south corridor for many animals, the northern limit of the distribution of some southern animals including Koklass Pheasant and masked civet, as well as the southern limit of the distribution of many representative animals of the north including hazel grouse and Remiz pendulinus. According to the statistics available as of April 30, 2022, the reserve harbors 1,870 species of advanced plants from 665 genera and 168 families, among which there is ginseng, the national first-class protected plant, walnut, the national second-class protected plant, and 8 kinds of national third-class protected plants including Juglans mandshurica, Glycine soja and Pteroceltis tatarinowii. 173 species of terrestrial vertebrates inhabit the reserve, among which 2 are national first-class protected animals, namely golden eagles and leopards, and 15 are second-class protected animals including vultures, colugos, and gorals. Mount Wuling is indeed a living museum presenting the past and the present of nature.

Mount Wuling National Nature Reserve, with a forest coverage of 93%, boasts its main landscape composed of forests, "skeletons" of green mountains and sharp peaks, "veins" of clear streams and lucid ponds, and cultural treasures dotting the ranges. A vivid picture of the harmony between static and dynamic elements as well as natural and cultural landscapes is presented by the reserve. Here mountains tower and overlap, quietly but grandly; streams trickle and meet, clear and bright; clouds drift and change, giving visitors a sense of dreaming; peaks and stones are like sculptures, spectacular and majestic. In spring everything comes back to life, with birds singing, willows sprouting, bees and butterflies twirling around, and azaleas, lilacs and honeysuckles blooming. Blazed with different colors and interspersed by green, the land showcases different shades of hues and layers. In summer, outside the mountain, everything is under the scorching sun; while in the mountain, shady trees grow vigorously and sway lightly in the cooling breezes. Gold-like globe-flowers and jade-like anemones scatter on the ground, sparkling and graceful; impressive waterfalls cascade down the mountainside, while streams and ponds keep running silently. In autumn, the green color at the foot of the mountain contrasts with the golden yellow birches and larches at the top. Aspens, Acer monos and China berries on the mountainside turn yellow, red and purple layer by layer. Looking out, patches of red leaves and bunches of fleshy fruits decorate the peaks and ridges, like lovely boats with billowing red sails floating on the blue waves, and the rosy clouds dispersing in the bright sky. In winter, all the lofty mountains and ranges are wrapped in a white snow blanket, with ice and icicles covering trees and branches. Pines and cypresses stand tall and straight with green leaves peeping up between heavy snow, presenting the typical northern climate and the chilly but elegant view of Mount Wuling.

Chapter 8
Yesanpo

—Treasure House of North China Canyon

Yesanpo National Geopark is mainly composed of eroded narrow gorges, fractured valleys, karst caves and springs, and forest landscapes. In terms of geological structure, Yesanpo is located at the junction of the fault and uplift zone of the Taihang Mountains and the fold zone of the Yanshan Mountains. The eroded narrow gorges are a kind of canyon landform formed by the long-term erosion and dissolution of the dissolvable rock mass developed from vertical fissures and joints.

Yesanpo National Geopark

野三坡国家地质公园

Yesanpo, as a national key scenic spot and national 5A-level tourist attraction, consists of more than 100 scenic spots and 7 scenic areas, namely Bai Li Gorge ("a hundred *li* gorge"), Juma River, Baicaopan Forest, Yugu Cave, Longmen Tianguan Great Wall Conservation Zone, Jinhua Mountain, and Yesanpo Lost Paradise Lavender Manor, all with different features and functions.

Bai Li Gorge, "the best gorge in the world", is the key scenic spot of Yesanpo. Almost all tourists to Yesanpo are amazed by its majesty, steepness, magic and serenity. In the canyon, strange rocks and sheer cliffs stand tall while trees and plants grow wild, forming "a hundred li gallery" of natural scenery with thick and heavy colors. The magical charm of the Bai Li Gorge mainly comes from its geomorphological type. On both sides of the canyon are the sky-high cliffs, straight up and straight down, and the valley wall and the bottom of the valley are almost vertical—seemingly sliced by knife and chopped by axe. And there lies a small amount of sediments in the bottom.

Considerable geomorphology and geological knowledge hide in Bai Li Gorge. The scenic spot "Wa xie dou zhi" (whose literal meaning is "frog and crab battle of wits") is made up of three large stones shaped like one frog and two crabs, whose scientific name is "collapsed rock block". Such formation of disaster geological relics is due to the vertical cracking in the rock; and by the effect of vibration or gravity, the rock blocks on the rock wall collapsed. The scenic spot "Yi xian tian" (whose literal meaning is "a thin strip of sky") represents the initial stage of the formation of peaks and valleys, which are formed by the widening of vertical crevasses caused by physical weathering, intermittent mountain torrents and lateral erosion. The stalactites on the walls of the peaks on both sides of the valley, known scientifically as "modern travertine", are the product of calcium carbonate deposits in the rocks. The flat boulders with wavy tracks in the middle of the road record the marks left on the surface of these loose, unconsolidated sediments by the waves in the lake-shore and coastal areas over a billion years ago. The scenic spot "Jin xian xuan zhen" (which means "golden thread hanging needle") is another surprise of the nature. In the deep and narrow rock wall cracks there sandwiches a huge rock, like a needle on the thread. Geological experts hold that the wonder was formed when the rocks was knocked down from the top of the mountain by geological movements or earthquakes hundreds of millions of years ago; the separated mountains were rejoined in the process, and the falling rocks were trapped in the middle.

Begonia Valley,
Baili Gorge
百里峡 海棠峪

Bai Li Gorge is just like a natural geology textbook unfolding all kinds of wonders competing for beauty. The Stone Sculpture Guanyin is a masterpiece of granite carved by nature. Groups of vertical cracks in the rock became rock pillars in the collapse process, and after long-term spherical weathering, the "head" and "neck" of "Guanyin" were formed as we see. The Tiger Spring close to the Stone Sculpture Guanyin is a typical fissure spring. Cracks emerged in the rock layer, and the water in the cracks penetrated downward and converged; when it met the barrier of the impervious rock layer below, the water stopped flowing and became a spring. The Tiancheng Bridge, a natural stone arched bridge in Bai Li Gorge, is 10 meters long, 2 meters wide, and 1.5 meters thick, with an 11-meter-high bridge opening. The piers of the bridge are composed of intrusive igneous rocks of 65 million years, while the bridge itself is formed by sedimentary dolomite of 1 billion years ago. Magma intrusion occurred 65 million years ago after the formation of dolomite, which later condensed and formed the current magmatic piers. Several groups of different directional cracks in the dolomite were developed, and about 700,000 years ago the crust uplifted. Through physical weathering, the dolomite began to peel off along the cracks and the joint planes. The Tiansheng Bridge, whose main structure and piers are composed of magmatic rock and dolomite, was formed by the erosion of running water.

In the Baili Gorge, a masterpiece of nature, people can not only enjoy the magnificent scenery, but also gain unexpected geographical and geological knowledge. People will genuinely feel the true beauty of nature when they carefully read the detailed descriptions of different geological landscapes during the tour.

The 70-li Juma River flows westward through Yesanpo. Along its two sides craggy peaks stand and steep rocks lie, while the clear water flows slowly by. Visitors can either take a boat to enjoy the scenery, or swim in the river and appreciate the spectacular nature. The white and soft sand dunes are ideal places for sand bathing and sunbathing. The resorts, the Hmong villages and the surrounding scenic spots integrate here, making it the best choice for leisure, entertainment, and summer stays.

The Longmen Tianguan Scenic Spot boasts mighty mountains, towering cliffs, clear springs and bubbling streams. Since ancient times, it has been the traffic artery leading from the capital to the Zijing Pass(a pass of the Great Wall), and also the battlefield for military strategists. The spot was regarded as a military fortress all through the Jin, Ming and Qing Dynasties, with numerous troops deployed to keep guard. Therefore, many cultural relics and scenic spots are left to this day, including the Great Longmen Castle, the Caishu'an section of the Great Wall, the Cliffside Carvings, etc. They are key cultural relic protection units of Hebei Province.

Deep canyons and lofty peaks render the Longmen Gorge grand and magnificent. Here the granites of the tectonic period of the Yanshan Mountains compose the strange and beautiful landform, presenting the vivid sights of Tian Quan Dai Yue (literally it means "a sky dog expecting the moon") Stone, Shen Shi (literally it means "a divine lion") Peak, Tianshi Jiang Ji (literally it means "a Taoist master is talking about the constellation named 'Ji'") Fish Scale Stone, Qianceng (literally it means "thousands of layers") Stone, etc. The famous Zijing Pass Fault Zone cuts through the granite mass, forming the Longmen Tianguan cliff. Along the gully fault gorge, fault fracture zones, fault scratches and fault mirrors can be seen. The development of multiple groups of granite joints, after long-term weathering erosion, contributed to the formation of multistage steep, with multi-stage waterfall cascading down in such a fairyland.

In the east and southeast of Yesanpo are limestone and dolomite, each layer of rock containing the fossils of marine animals during its formation. If you have a chance to visit Yesanpo and take a look at the exposed layers, you will notice that most of them are uneven and pleated, because at the beginning of the formation process the earth's crust subsided and received the deposits of various materials; and in the later period, the sediments were compressed and thus corrugated. In addition, many of the rocks here show regular "ripple marks" left by waves on the surface of soft sediments when the rocks were originally formed.

Baicaopan Forest Resort Area, with an altitude of 1,983 meters, is the commanding peak of Yesanpo. Here, mountains stand straight with grotesque peaks and rocks; wild flowers bloom here and there, and flocks of wild animals are everywhere in large numbers. The thickness and denseness of the forest renders this area "the green pearl" of the Taihang

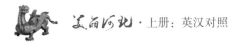

Mountains. Climbing the Shicheng (literally it means "stony city") Ridge to appreciate the sunrise and the sea of clouds, coming to the Mayi (literally it means "ants") Ridge to explore red ant nests, listening to the soughing of the wind in the pines at the Fengdong (literally it means "vibrating in wind") Stone, and enjoying thousands of mu of azaleas and endless stretches of forests, tourists always enjoy themselves so much that they don't want to leave.

🂡 Chapter 9
Zhangshiyan

—Three Ancient Roads Connecting Nine Valleys, Eight Spots Hidden in Four Scenic Areas

The 800-li Taihang Mountains is one of the hottest spots in Hebei Province—not for its height but for its eye-popping scenery presenting horizontally, with its cliffs as long as the Great Wall surprising people continuously. In the evolution of nature, the Taihang Mountains has formed a unique geological landform, the most representative of which is Zhangshiyan landform, equally famous as karst landform and Danxia landform.

The Zhihutao Scenic Spot of Zhangshiyan National Geological Park (hereafter referred to as "Zhangshiyan"), which is located in Zanhuang County, is about 100 kilometers from the

Zhangshiyan landform
嶂石岩地貌

provincial capital Shijiazhuang. This scenic spot boasts the most famous iconic landscape of Zhangshiyan—Chibi Danya. The colorful cliff has been standing there for thousands of years. In the morning light, the color of the cliff changes from brilliant red to bright yellow, and then gradually to gray. Such a spectacular view is described by Qiao Yu (a poet of the Ming Dynasty) in his poem as: "On the wall of the towering cliff, many different colors change in the sunlight, which looks like flowers blooming in the midair when seen from a distance. The vibrant red cliff and the green color of the surrounding plants add radiance to each other, which is even more beautiful than the masterpiece of Wang Wei's landscape painting."

Integrating the lofty, bold, precipitous, pristine and majestic nature of the Taihang Mountains, Zhangshiyan creates a montage of visions with the three-dimensional space composed of height, breadth and depth of the red cliff as well as the clouds, mist and green plants.

Zhangshiyan, originally little known, was discovered during a geological investigation. In 1972, Guo Kang, a researcher from Hebei Institute of Geography, discovered a magnificent sandstone landform featuring stretching red cliff during his investigation of the Taihang Mountains. After years of investigation and research, the landform was officially named "Zhangshiyan landform". It is one of the three sandstone landforms in China (the other two are Danxia landform and Zhangjiajie landform), and is a representative section of the grandeur and magnificent Taihang Mountains. This landform has five characteristics: Danya cliff stretching horizontally and continuously, steeped cliffs existing everywhere, Ω-shaped valleys connecting with each other, block-structured boulders showing sharp edges and corners, and rock walls of the valleys extending vertically from the bottom to the top. Zhangshiyan boasts a large number of striking geological and geomorphic landscapes and rich historical and local cultural scenic spots, which convey the concept that man is an integral part of nature and add even more brilliance to the land.

Zhangshiyan, located in the middle part of the Taihang Mountains, belongs to the west wing of the northward-overturned anticline in Zanhuang with its axial from south to north. It also forms the main ridge of the Taihang Mountains with Mesoproterozoic Changchengian sandstone covered by Paleozoic Cambrian limestone. The attitude of the stratum is relatively gentle while the vertical fissure is rather developed; thin layers of claystone are sandwiched by thick sandstone, and cases of block collapse, erosion and denudation arise commonly. The landform showcases unusually steep terrain with all types of landscapes and stunning views, thus it was named as the "Zhangshiyan landform".

Zhangshiyan landscape is mainly composed of Danya (red cliffs), wall ridges, sharp peaks and deep valleys, whose characteristics can be roughly summarized as "three ancient roads connecting nine valleys, while eight scenic spots hidden in four barrier-like scenic areas (namely Jiunü Peak, Yuantong Temple, Zhihutao and Donglingbei, which are relatively independent to each other)". The eight scenic spots are dotted in the four scenic areas: Jiu Xian Ju Hui (九仙聚会 , literally it means "nine fairies gathering together"), Yan Ban Gua Gong (岩半花宫 , literally it means "flowers blooming in the midair"), Qing Tian Fei Yu (晴天飞雨 , literally it means "raindrops flying in sunshine"), Hui Ying Ju Ya (回音巨崖 , literally it means "giant echo cliff"), Huai Quan Liang Yi (淮泉凉意 , literally it means "pleasant coolness of Huai Spring"), Dongling Yu Zhu (冻凌玉柱 , literally it means "jade-like icicles of Donglingbei"), Chong Men Suo Cui (重门锁翠 , literally it means "emerald-like vegetation surrounded by giant cliffs"), Die Zhang Xuan Zhong (叠嶂悬钟 , literally it means "a bell-like towering peak surrounded by many mountains"). The three ancient roads, the nine valleys, the four scenic areas including the eight scenic spots are all interconnected by narrow pathways, linking the total 120 scenic spots together. Among them, Hui Ying Ju Ya, Dongling Yu Zhu, the Misty Cave, and the Buddha Light are called the "four wonders of Zhangshiyan", while Qing Tian Fei Yu, Shi Ru Ling Quan (石乳灵泉 , literally it means "magic milk dripping from a suspending stalactite"), Yun Ya Sa Zhu (云崖撒珠 ,literally it means "beads-like water drops falling down from the towering cliff"),Yin Pu Luo Hu (银瀑落湖 , literally it means "silver waterfall falling into the lake") are regarded as the "four wonders of the water view of Zhangshiyan".

Travelling through Zhangshiyan's fascinating scenic spots, visitors will truly feel the beauty of nature. But to really appreciate the charm in depth, one should first know how the landform is formed—only by understanding the causes of its formation can we fully unveil the most magical aspect of Zhangshiyan.

The vast expanse of the red brocades of Zhangshiyan is called "long cliff" in geology. Long cliffs are the products of the mountain planation surfaces being cut, or the products of faults. After natural cutting and destruction, the cliffs have become what they look like today. Their length can reach as long as dozens of meters to hundreds of meters, so do their height. The long cliffs are usually so steep on both sides that they look like long huge walls, thus they are also called "broken walls". Such a geological feature is particularly obvious in the north of the Donglingbei area. From long cliffs to broken walls is a natural process of change and development. With the passage of time and geological changes, broken walls are further divided and destroyed, forming the geological landscapes such as mesas, pillars and towers. As to mesas, Huangannao scenic spot is rather typical, and as to towers, Jiunü Peak is rather typical. The steep

Zhangshiyan landform
嶂石岩地貌

red long cliff seen by tourists in Zhangshiyan comprises mainly of red quartzite with its bedrock bare on one side. It consists of three overlapping layers, with two platforms, known locally as "Zhan" ("stacks") between each of the two layers. Fallen stones of all sizes are piled up on the two stacks. And in midsummer, bushes and grass overgrow among the stones. These two stacks are like two jasper belts winding along the long cliff and making the long cliff more spectacular and beautiful.

If the landscape represented by the long cliff is one style of Zhangshiyan, then the unique set of Ω-shaped narrow gorges display another completely different style of it. The representative of the Ω-shaped narrow gorges is the Echo Wall located in the Echo Valley, which is also known as the Echo Cliff and was listed in the Guinness World Record in 1997. Shaped like a semicircle, or more specifically, the letter Ω, the Echo Wall possesses a diameter of 90 meters, an arc of 250 degrees, and an arc length of 300 meters. No matter where you stand shouting in the valley, the voice reflected back can be heard clearly. Rising here and subsiding there, the tourists' voices echo in the mountains.

As a shining pearl of the Taihang Mountains, Zhangshiyan is indeed the prime site of it. When you plan to visit the Taihang Mountains, you should not miss the magnificence of Zhangshiyan. The more you know about it, the more you will find it attractive.

Chapter 10
Hengshui Lake

—Yan-Zhao's Most Beautiful Wetland, a Paradise for Birds

"In the lake, reeds are waving and lotus flowers are blooming; ducks are playing, and gulls and egrets are in the sky soaring." When talking about Hengshui Lake, the poem naturally comes into people's mind.

October is the best season to visit Hengshui Lake, which enjoys many reputations such as "the sapphire in East Asia", "the most beautiful wetland in Beijing Tianjin and Hebei", and "the most spectacular lake to the south of Beijing". In October, it is in its most refreshing and comfortable days.

Hengshui Lake
衡水湖

Located on the north side of Jizhou City of Hengshui, which is in the central and southern part of North China Plain, Hengshui Lake National Nature Reserve is a renowned lake wetland in Hebei Province. It covers an area of 187.87 square kilometers, including vast lakes, dense reeds, lotus ponds and mid-lake islands. Its biodiversity is very rich, and it is the home of inland freshwater wetland animals and species of birds under national class I and class II protection; elegant cranes, beautiful swans, swift gulls and nimble egrets can always be seen swimming leisurely or flying happily.

In 602 B.C., the Yellow River breached and changed its course, forming the "one thousand qing [qing, a unit of area (=6.6667 hectares)] of depression" with water all year around. Covering a total area of 120 square kilometers, including 19 square kilometers of deep water area, Hengshui Lake, known as "Jiangnan of the north", fills our minds with picturesque images such as blue waves rolling and fishermen rowing and singing in the sunset. Water from the Wei Canal, the Yellow River and the Yangtze River are collected here, so Hengshui Lake deserves the honor as "containing the water from the Yangtze River and the Yellow River in one lake".

The nature reserve belongs to the warm temperate monsoon continental climate zone, with four distinct seasons. The annual average temperature measures 13.0°C and the annual rainfall amounts to 518.9 millimeters. The superior natural environment makes the place suitable for the survival and reproduction of wild animals and plants, with 370 species of plants, 194 species of insects, 26 species of fish, 17 species of amphibious reptiles, 296 species of birds, 17 species of mammals, 201 species of phytoplankton, 174 species of zooplankton and 23 species of benthic animals growing and living here. Among the wild animals and plants, the wetland boasts its birds the most, with 7 species of national class I protected birds, including red-crowned cranes, white cranes, black storks, oriental white storks, great bustards, golden eagles and eastern imperial eagles, as well as 44 species of national class II protected birds, including whooper swans, cygnets and gray cranes. Every year, hundreds of thousands of summer migratory birds, mainly whiskered terns and black-winged stilts, nest and breed here; more than 3,000 grey cranes and tens of thousands of geese overwinter at the wetland, and white-cheeked

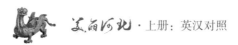

starlings covering all the sky form a unique breathtaking scene.

Carrying out the functions of flood storage, drought prevention, climate regulation, soil erosion control, and environmental pollution abatement, Hengshui Lake not only benefits the locals but also mediates the climate changes and improves the ecological environment in the surrounding areas and even some places of Beijing and Tianjin. It is also the regulation and storage water source of South-to-North Water Diversion Project, providing drinking water and industrial and agricultural water for Hengshui and its surrounding cities and contributing to the regional economic development. In a word, Hengshui Lake confers considerable benefits in terms of ecology, society and economy.

The nature reserve is situated in the Economic Circle around Beijing and Tianjin, the Bohai Rim Economic Circle, the Yellow River Economic Cooperation Zone and the Northeast Asia Economic Circle. Within the circumference of 300 kilometers, there lie two municipalities of Beijing and Tianjin, four provincial capitals of Shijiazhuang, Taiyuan, Zhengzhou and Jinan, and 26 prefecture-level cities. Its obvious location advantage, distinctive wetland resources, picturesque natural scenery and profound history and culture endow the reserve with exceptional merit in ecotourism. To this end, according to the principle of "protection, development, utilization and again protection" with biodiversity conservation as the

Water Birds in Hengshui Lake
衡水湖中的水鸟

core, ecological popular science tourism as the feature, and the sustainable utilization of natural resources and sustainable economic development as the goal, the government will undertake wetland restoration at West Lake and Fuyangxin River, open up new waters and expand the area of wetlands based on the South-to-North Water Diversion Project, improve ecological environment through the construction of water conservation forests, excavate and develop historical and cultural resources and accelerate the construction of ecotourism infrastructure and ecological service areas, strengthen biodiversity protection in the core and buffer areas and promote the development of ecological science popularization tourism and other related industries in the experimental and demonstration areas. Hengshui Lake will thus grow into a national nature reserve with supportive environment, sufficient resources and developed economy where people live happily, and a demonstration area of wetland protection at home and abroad for wetland protection, economic development, and sustainable utilization of natural resources.

Hengshui Lake National Nature Reserve is not only rich in biodiversity and beautiful natural scenery, but also possesses far-reaching history and culture. The ancient city of Jizhou, located on the south bank of Hengshui Lake, was built in the sixth year of the reign of Emperor Gaozu of the Han Dynasty (201 B.C.) and won the reputation as "the first of the nine states". There are many historical sites and legends in this area, such as the Great Wall of the Han Dynasty and the Ming Dynasty, ancient tombs and stone monuments of the Han Dynasty, the stone mill of Li Sanniang[1], the legend of Zhulin Temple flying up to heaven … , which demonstrate the mystery and beauty of the natural, historical and cultural landscapes of Hengshui Lake.

---

[1] the stone mill of Li Sanniang: a famous queen during the period of the Five Dynasties and Ten Kingdoms.

Chapter 11
Bashang Grasslands

—The World of Grass and the Ocean of Flowers

"Bashang" is a geographical term, which specifically refers to an area of meadow grassland formed by the steep rise of the terrain and the influence of the climate and vegetation. Here this term generally refers to the region located within 100 kilometers north of Zhangjiakou and Chengde, including Zhangbei, Shangyi, Kangbao, and Guyuan counties in Zhangjiakou, Fengning and Weichang counties of Chengde, as well as Hexigten Banner and Duolun County in Inner Mongolia Autonomous Region, with a total area of more than 200,000 square kilometers.

As an important part of the Inner Mongolia Plateau, the Bashang region, in terms of tourist destinations, is mainly divided into four areas, namely, Weichang Bashang (Mulan Paddock),

Bashang Grassland
坝上草原

Fengning Bashang, Zhangbei Bashang and Guyuan Bashang. Among them, Mulan Paddock-Ulan Butong Grassland is the most beautiful, but also the farthest from Beijing. As a part of Inner Mongolia Grassland, Bashang Grassland covers a total area of about 350 square kilometers of Hebei Province; Kangbao Grassland next to Inner Mongolia presents the most genuine Inner Mongolian Grassland style. The average elevation of Bashang Grassland is 1,486 meters, and the highest elevation is about 2,400 meters. It is the birthplace of the Luanhe River and the Chaohe River. The vast green fields bloomed with flowers stretch into the distance, and the sky and clouds seem so close to the ground. During the tourism season, the average temperature of Bashang Grassland is 17.4 °C, making it an ideal tourist and leisure resort.

High in the southeast and low in the northwest, the topography of Bashang Grassland is characterized by hills and plains, dotted with dense rivers and lakes. The plateau grassland reaches between 1,200 meters and 1,400 meters above sea level. Along the grassland, there are lots of passes and peaks, the highest of which is over 2,500 meters above sea level. Categorized as the continental monsoon climate, Bashang Grassland displays the characteristics of being cold, windy and arid. The average annual temperature here is 1−2 °C, the average frost-free period is 90−120 days, and the annual precipitation is about 400 millimeters.

The scenery of Bashang Grassland is its most eye-catching part. In summer, green grass rustle under the blue sky; colorful flowers bloom everywhere, and the air is filled with a fresh fragrance. In autumn, the mountains are dressed in red, and the fragrance of wild fruits fills the air. In winter, it becomes a wonderland of ice covered in thick snow. No poem or picture can fully express its exquisite beauty.

Bashang Grassland is a typical arid grassland (called "Caotan" by locals). There are mainly drought-resistant grasses on the grassland, with the grass height of 15−40 centimeters. This type of grassland occupies a large part of the plateau grassland. Meadow grassland is the best type of all the grasslands, which can be seen frequently in some scenic areas such as the Wuhua Meadow, the Shandian Riverside, and the Chabei Pasture, which are all in Guyuan County, as well as the most scenic areas in Weichang County and part of the Datan Scenic Area in Fengning

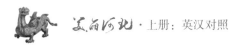

County. In these places, perennial herbaceous plants measuring 30—60 centimeters high are the major plants, with a variety of wildflowers blooming as well.

Natural forests in Bashang are mainly distributed in the area of Saihanba in Weichang, southeast of Guyuan, and the areas bordering Bashang in Fengning. Natural forests are mainly composed of white birch, poplar and apricot trees, while shrubs forests include shrubs of the elm family, willow family and bean family. The eastern part of the artificial forest is dominated by pines, and the western part by poplars. Generally speaking, the forest coverage varies from 8% to 12%. In Mulan Paddock National Forest Park, which is in the eastern part of Bashang, its forest coverage has reached 30% to 70% or even more, distinguishing here with better ecological environment. However, the western part is generally characterized by deserts with some artificial forests. The forest coverage of Bashang directly affects the ecological environment around Beijing. The rivers in Bashang are mostly inland, seasonal and often dry. In the rainy season, torrential floods and rivers gather together and form "nur" meaning "lake" in Mongolian, among which the largest are seated in the territory of Shangyi and Zhangbei, namely "Chahan Nur" and "Anguli Nur". The largest out-flowing river is the Luanhe River, which originates in Fengning and flows through Guyuan, Zhenglan Banner, Duolun, then it flows back to Fengning and then flows through Weichang, etc. The part in Guyuan is called the "Shandian River", the part in Zhenglan Banner is called the "Shangdu River", and the part after it flows through Weichang is called "the Luanhe River". There are hundreds of natural nurs and reservoirs in Bashang, and the larger ones include the Chahan Nur in Shang Yi, the Anguli Nur and the Huanggai Nur in Zhang Bei, the Shandian River reservoir in Guyuan, the wetland in Fengning, and the Moon Lake and the General Paozi ("Paozi" is a dialect, meansing "a small lake") in Weichang. These waters are home to wild fish species—mainly crucian carps and common carps. Wetlands are distributed around reservoirs and nurs, with lake water billowing, lush grasses swaying, and swans and magpies singing.

Bashang Grassland is an important part of Bashang Plateau, boasting good ecological environment with clear water, lush vegetation and flocks

Lightning River, Guyuan County, Zhangjiakou
张家口沽源县闪电河

of Mongolian gazelles. In Mongolian, it is called "Hailiutu", referring to a place with abundant water and grass. On Bashang Grassland, the sky is high, the weather is pleasant, with soft green grass carpeting the ground, groups of horses scattering everywhere, and cattle and sheep flocking like clouds. At the edge of Bashang, steep peaks are majestic like clusters of arrows, with streams babbling between them. At the bordering areas between the plateau and the plain, the forests are dense, mountain delicacies are abundant, and wild animals can be seen everywhere. Once you step on the land of Bashang, you enter a world where you can fully enjoy the comfort of summer, with a cool breeze blowing gently on your face. Looking around, the land of lush green meadow is dotted with a variety of stars-like wild flowers. Brilliant sunlight filters through large tracts of birch forests, while the beautiful Shandian River flows by like a silk ribbon. Cattle, horses and sheep flocking here and there foraging in groups, shepherds singing with their sonorous voices, crisp sound of whip spreading in the air, as well as the melodious sounds of birds, all add infinite vitality to the unadorned grassland.

The summer air of Bashang is fresh and pleasant, and there is no scorching days in summer. The colorful wildflowers start at the edge of the plateau, some as brilliant as the twinkling stars, others as slender as red hairpins. The flowers vary in color throughout the seasons, and even during a day. In mornings and evenings, the colors of the flowers are also different. At night, the moonlight and bonfire create a romantic atmosphere. You can sit around the bonfire and talk with your loved ones, or talk, dance and sing with other tourists from all over the world; you can also sit alone on the grassland and enjoy the time of being alone. In the morning, after waking up, you can step on the soft grass, listen to the birds singing, or watch the sunrise over the horizon. When the red sun rises, the dewdrops on the green leaves immediately turn into twinkling pearls, various plants suddenly turn green, and horses, cattle and sheep start to move in the vast grassland, composing a scene just as what is described in a poem that "The sky is with a blue color, and the grassland has no border. In the wind, the grass seems lower, and the cattle feel free to wander".

 **Exercises**

Ⅰ. Comprehension

（1）After reading this part, would you please explain your views on the landform characteristics of Hebei?

（2）Baiyangdian Lake and Hengshui Lake both are wetlands. What are the differences between them?

（3）Among the three major landscape sandstone landforms in China, which kind is uniquely owned by Hebei? How is it distributed?

（4）After reading this division, please give a list of the geographical landforms of Hebei that are not included in this part.

Ⅱ. Translation

1. Term Translation

（1）红日浴海

（2）蛙蟹斗智

（3）赤壁丹崖

（4）溪光映带

2. Passage Translation

在中国，岛、关、河都可以作为市的名字，比如山东青岛市、甘肃嘉峪关市、河南漯河市。新中国成立初期，秦皇岛和山海关都是市，北戴河就更厉害了，民间称之为"都"（夏都）。所以，一些对地理陌生的人会觉得秦皇岛是北戴河下属的一个岛，也就不奇怪了。正本清源，秦皇岛才是河北省东北部的地级市，山海关、北戴河都是秦皇岛市下辖的区。秦皇岛市政府驻地为海港区，这个海港是秦皇岛港。

Part Three

Ancient Cities with Picturesque Views

Cities, bearing the heritage of history while witnessing the vicissitudes of the world, are the creations of the people who have lived here for thousands of years, and they are the immortal crystallization of the profound history and culture of this land. To understand the local culture, one should first know more about these ancient cities. For Hebei, there are six national historical and cultural cities, including Chengde, Baoding, Zhengding, Shanhaiguan Pass, Handan, and Yuxian, as well as six provincial historical and cultural cities, including Xuanhua, Zhuozhou, Dingzhou, Zhaoxian, Xingtai, and Daming. These ancient cities like sparkling pearls dotted on the land of Yan-Zhao, attracting tourists from all over the world with their unique charm and telling the world about the long history and splendid culture of Hebei Province.

Lead-in Questions

(1) What do you know about the historical and cultural heritage of the millennium-old counties in Hebei?

(2) Based on Chapter zf "The Historical Development of Hebei" in Part One, please discuss the origins of these national historical and cultural cities in Hebei.

(3) Which of Hebei's historical and cultural ancient cities have you visited?

(4) Which city in Hebei marked the beginning of China's urban planning? What impact did the design pattern of the central axis have on the architectural layout of later cities?

Jimingyi Ancient Town, Huailai County, Zhangjiakou

张家口怀来县鸡鸣驿古镇

Chapter 12
Chengde

—The Summer Resort and Hunting Ground of the Qing Dynasty Royals

Chengde, formerly known as "Rehe", is located in the transitional area between North China and Northeast China. It is close to Beijing and Tianjin, backed by Inner Mongolia and Liaoning, and adjacent to the coastal cities of Qinhuangdao and Tangshan, as well as Zhangjiakou City within Hebei. It is one of the first 24 national historical and cultural cities, one of China's top ten scenic spots, one of China's top 40 tourist attractions, one of the national key scenic spots, and one of the national first-class open cities. In 1994, Chengde Mountain Resort and its surrounding temples were approved by UNESCO as a world cultural heritage site, making Chengde a world-famous cultural city. In 2012, Chengde was listed as one of China's top ten characteristic leisure cities.

Chengde has a profound cultural heritage. The "Hongshan Culture" is a historical culture relic in Chengde in the Neolithic period, which dates back more than 5,000 years ago. During the transition from the clan society to the agricultural society in the late Neolithic period, nomadic

Overlooking Chengde City
俯瞰承德市

people from the Mongolian Plateau migrated along rivers into the plain area and passed through the Rehe region. Thus, Chengde had witnessed the evolution and development of Chinese people in the history. The culture at that period is known as the Yanshan Culture, which, along with the Yan-Zhao Culture, became the main historical and cultural heritages of Hebei.

During the Spring and Autumn Period and the Warring States Period, Chengde was under the jurisdiction of the three prefectures set by the Yan State, namely Yuyang, Youbeiping, and Liaoxi. According to the chapter "The Account of the Xiongnu" of *Records of the Grand Historian of China*[1], the Yan State once built the Great Wall in this area, and the remains of the ancient Great Wall can still be seen today. The discovery of the famous agricultural tools iron moulds in Xinglong County in Chengde indicates that agricultural production in this area was already quite developed at that time. After the Qin and Han Dynasties, central governments of all dynasties had set up administrative institutions here. In the long history of feudal society, the economic and cultural development of various ethnic groups such as the Han, Xiongnu (Hun), Wuhuan, Xianbei, Kumoxi, Qidan (Khitan), Turkic, and Mongolian in this area has been further promoted.

After the establishment of the Qing Dynasty, China's unified multi-ethnic national political power was further consolidated. Under the historical conditions at that time, the geographical location of Rehe became increasingly important. It is adjacent to Beijing and Tianjin, faces Zhangjiakou on the west, connects with Liaoning on the east, borders Inner Mongolia on the north, and neighbors Tangshan on the south. It is an important regional city in the hinterland of the Yanshan Mountains and on the coast of the Bohai Sea. Due to the natural conditions such as its pleasant climate and rich natural resources, it is an ideal place to build a summer resort and an important place to contact Mongolia to consolidate the border defense. Therefore, from the 42nd year of the Kangxi reign (1703 AD), Emperor Kangxi began to build the Chengde Mountain Resort, which was not completed until the 57th year of the Qianlong reign (1792

---

① Translated by Burton Watson found on https://www.cuhk.edu.hk/rct/toc/toc_historian.html.

AD). After its establishment, seven emperors of the Qing Dynasty had stopped over at this resort. Over a period of more than 150 years, this resort experienced a tortuous process of prosperity, decline, and revival. During the Kangxi and Qianlong reigns of the Qing Dynasty, it was a period of prosperity for Chengde Mountain Resort and the Eight Outer Temples. Emperors stayed here to govern during the summer, making it the second political center of the country. With the decline of the Qing Dynasty, the once prosperous Chengde Mountain Resort and the Eight Outer Temples began to decline. As an important political center in the Qing Dynasty, Chengde had gathered leaders and ministers of various ethnic groups of the dynasty. It is now home to one of China's three major ancient architectural complexes, the Chengde Mountain Resort and the Eight Outer Temples. In 1976, the State Council approved *The First Ten-Year Plan for the Renovation of the Chengde Mountain Resort and the Eight Outer Temples*, which allowed for the large-scale renovation of the resort and the Eight Outer Temples.

The ancient city of Chengde is a national historical and cultural city in China that integrates royal culture, ancient architectural culture, Buddhist culture, and Central Plains Confucian culture.

In addition to the Chengde Mountain Resort and the Eight Outer Temples, the nationally protected cultural relics in Chengde also include the City God Temple (Chenghuang Temple) and the Jinshanling Great Wall.

The City God Temple of Chengde, also known as the "Rehe Capital City God Temple" designated by Emperor Qianlong, is located in the center of Chengde City, on the north side of the West Street, about 1 kilometer away from the Chengde Mountain Resort. It is a typical Han-style temple with a simple layout. The yellow glazed roof of the City God Temple is decorated with colorful ornaments, intentionally or unintentionally displaying its unique position among the city god temples in various places. There are nearly 90 statues in the temple. The main building, Fuyin Yanjiang Hall ("Fuyin Yanjiang" means "good fortune covering all the country"), enshrines a seated statue of the City God, which has a benevolent appearance and is known as the "Number One City God in the Country". It is said that the City God is Yunli, the seventeenth prince of Emperor Kangxi. Yunli was open-minded and knowledgeable since childhood, and did not participate in the struggle for imperial power. Moreover, he was intelligent and prudent, with outstanding capabilities. After his death, Emperor Qianlong deeply felt the loss of a great helper. In the 37th year of Qianlong reign (1772 AD), Zhou Yuanli, the Minister of Works, requested to build the City God Temple of Rehe. Emperor Qianlong issued an edict to allocate funds for the construction and conferred Yunli as the City God of Rehe.

The Jinshanling Great Wall is a section of the Great Wall built during the Ming Dynasty. It stretches across the Yanshan Mountains' branch range, located at the border of Luanping County of Hebei Province and Miyun District of Beijing. It starts from the historically famous Gubeikou Pass in the west and extends to the towering Wangjing Tower in the east, with a total length of 10.5 kilometers. Along the wall, there are 5 passes, 67 watchtowers, and 2 beacon towers. The Jinshanling Great Wall is famous for its open views, dense watchtowers, unique landscape,

Mulan Autumn
Hunting
清雍正 粉彩木兰
秋狝大盘

exquisite architectural art, complete military defense system, and well-preserved condition. In addition, there are unique landscapes: the fantastic architecture of "Wangjing Tower", the thrilling spectacle of "Shoulüji", the towering "Stairway to Heaven", the world-famous "Wall with Characters", hot springs, the Tianquan (a spring on the halfway up the Tiger Mountain), the Turtle-like Stone, the Tongtian Hole, the large Jinshan Tower and the small Jinshan Tower, etc. The Jinshanling Great Wall can be regarded as the quintessence of the Great Wall of China. Compared to the internationally renowned Badaling Great Wall, it is equally impressive, and it is an excellent tourist attraction.

In 1987, it was listed as a world cultural heritage site, and it is a national key cultural relics protection unit, a national scenic spot, and a national 4A-level tourist attraction.

Mulan Paddock, also known as Saihanba National Forest Park, has a full name of "Saihandabahanseqin" in Mongolian, which means "beautiful ridge with rivers". In 1681, Emperor Kangxi of the Qing Dynasty established a hunting ground of more than 10,000 square kilometers here to train the army. In the first half of the Qing Dynasty, the emperors would lead princes, ministers, and elite soldiers of the Eight Banners to this place every year to hold activities mainly focused on hunting and tourism, historically known as "Mulan Autumn Hunting".

▨ Chapter 13

Baoding

—The Southern Gate of China's Capital City Beijing

The word "Baoding" first appeared in the poem *The Royalty* in the section of "Book of Odes" in *Book of Poetry*[1], meaning "blessing and stability". It can be seen as an expression of ancient people's hope and longing for a better life.

Gate of the capital city and its environs

京畿之门

---

[1] This book is translated by Xu Yuanchong and published in 1993.

With the Taihang Mountains as a barrier to the west and the Baiyang dian Lake to the east, Baoding, which is easy to defend and difficult to attack, has always been a strategically important location for military purposes due to its geographical position of "controlling three passes in the north, reaching nine provinces to the south, connecting four regions, and dominating the Central Plains". During the Northern Song Dynasty, to strengthen the northern border defense, the "Bao Sai Army" was established in Qingyuan County (today's Qingyuan District of Baoding). "Bao Sai" means "defending the border". In the third year of the Chunhua reign of the Northern Song Dynasty (992 AD), Baozhou City was built, marking the start of Baoding City's history of more than 1,000 years.

As time passed by, in the 22nd year of the reign of Emperor Taizu of the Yuan Dynasty (1227 AD), Zhang Rou (a native of Dingxing County of Baoding), a great general under Genghis Khan, "designed the layout, settled the people, channeled water into the city, and restored the city Baozhou", laying the foundation for the layout of today's Baoding City, which takes on the boot-like structure.

In 1272, the Yuan Dynasty established its capital in Dadu (today's Beijing). While laying the foundation for Beijing's urban layout, its political influence also radiated to the surrounding areas. The formerly single-function military Baozhou then became the seat of the political center of Shuntian Lu (Lu, a term of administrative division in the Yuan Dynasty) and began to take on political functions. In 1275, Shuntian Lu was renamed Baoding Lu, serving as the southern gate of Dadu. The implication of the word "Baoding"—"defending Dadu and stabilizing the country"—may have originated from this time.

During the Ming Dynasty, Baoding Lu was changed to Baoding Prefecture. The biggest change during this period was that, to meet the needs of defense, the city walls of Baoding were transformed from earthen walls to brick walls. In the 11th year of Chongzhen reign of the Ming Dynasty (1638 AD), the Governor-general of Baoding was established, governing the areas of Baoding, Shandong, Tianjin, and Denglai, and later expanded to include parts of Huguang (today's Hunan and Hubei), holding significant power.

During the Qing Dynasty, there were nine high-ranking officials known as the "nine governor-generals" who were in charge of various regions. The governor-general of Zhili was in charge of Zhili Province. Due to its strategic location in the capital region, the governor-general of Zhili held significant power. The area under the governor-general of Zhili's jurisdiction roughly covered today's Tianjin, as well as most of Hebei Province, a small part of Henan Province, and a small part of Shandong Province.

The saying "The governor-general's office reflect half of the Qing Dynasty's history" not only highlights the great power of the governor-general of Zhili, but also serves as a witness to the prosperity of Baoding, the capital of Zhili Province. Though the average term of the post was 2.5 years, Li Hongzhang, also known as the "Bismarck of the East", however held the post for 25 years, while also serving as the "Three-title Teacher of the Eastern Palace" (a honorary title for high-rank officials tutoring the crown prince), the Grand Secretary of the Wenhua Palace, and the Minister of Beiyang Commerce, wielding great power in the court. As the residence of the head of the nine governor-generals, Baoding experienced a rapid leap forward in the development of politics, economy, culture and other aspects.

Baoding Prefecture was first built more than 600 years ago during the Hongwu reign of the Ming Dynasty. Today, the most well-preserved ancient provincial government office in China, the Zhili Governor-general's Office, is located in the center of the ancient city, with the famous Ancient Lotus Pond Garden, one of the top ten famous gardens in the country, nearby. The Daci Pavilion, which was built during the Yuan Dynasty, is one of the "eight scenic spots of Shanggu (Shanggu, the name for Baoding in ancient times)". The solemn and magnificent Western Imperial Tombs of the Qing Dynasty in Yixian County, the ancient and dignified Mancheng Tombs of the Han Dynasty, the heroic and tragic atmosphere of the ancient Yishui River Site and the Yanxiadu (the second capital of Yan State) ruins, the ruins of the underground battlefield of the Song Dynasty in Xiongxian County once resounding with the sounds of war drums and horns, the Ranzhuang Tunnel Warfare Site that demonstrates the Chinese nation's upright spirit, and the Langya Mountain Five Heroes Memorial Tower, all these natural and cultural landscapes form a colorful and diverse tourism area with unique characteristics.

The Ancient Lotus Pond Garden is located in the downtown area of

The Ancient Lotus Pond
古莲花池

Baoding. Known as the "Garden of Blooms in the Summer Ripples (涟
漪夏艳)", the Ancient Lotus Pond Garden is one of the eight scenic spots
of Baoding, a national-level cultural relics protection unit, and one of the
top ten famous gardens in China. The garden was first built during the
reign of Emperor Gaozong of the Tang Dynasty and was later renovated
and expanded during the Yuan and Ming Dynasties. In the eleventh year
of Yongzheng's reign of the Qing Dynasty (1733), Li Wei, the governor-
general of Zhili, established an academy in the garden according to the
imperial order, which attracted numerous talents and gained fame both
at home and abroad. Later, it became an imperial palace, and emperors
and empresses such as Qianlong, Jiaqing, and Dowager Cixi stayed here
during their tours when passing through Baoding.

The Daci Pavilion is located on the Yuhua West Road, and is
adjacent to the Ancient Lotus Pond Garden. It is a representative work of
ancient architecture and a symbol of Baoding, the national historical and
cultural city. There is a saying, "If you haven't been to the Daci Pavilion,
you haven't been to Baoding." The Daci Pavilion, originally named
"Dabei Pavilion", was built by Zhang Rou, the Duke of Cai of the Yuan

Dynasty[1]. It ranks first among all the "eight scenic spots" of Baoding, historically known as "the City Pavilion Reaching the Sky (市阁凌霄)". The Daci Pavilion is 31 meters tall, with 22 steps in front of it. Inside the pavilion, the statue of Guanyin Bodhisattva stands on a lotus petal-shaped base, looking serene. The Guanyin statue is made of wood, 5.5 meters high, with 42 arms holding various ritual implements. On both sides of the pavilion, there are murals depicting the eighteen Arhats and stories from the sutras, which are works from the late Qing Dynasty. Each figure has a unique expression, and they are artistic treasures of the pavilion. Inside the pavilion, the caisson ceiling and beams are decorated with Xuanzi colored paintings[2]. There is a corridor surrounding the pavilion, and when looking down from here, the city streets and residential houses can be clearly seen. The pavilion has three floors. Climbing up to the third floor and looking out the window, you can get a superb panorama of the western mountains including their faint peaks.

The Daci Pavilion
大慈阁

① "Cai" is an ancient state. It was common to honor a duke by adding the name of an ancient state to the title of "duke" at that time
② "Xuanzi colored painting" is a kind of color painting style in ancient Chinese architecture, which can be widely seen in royal palaces and nobles' mansions.

As a national historical and cultural city, Baoding has a profound cultural heritage and glorious revolutionary tradition. As early as the fourth year of Xining reign of the Northern Song Dynasty (1091), the "Zhou School"[1] was established in the Ancient Lotus Pond Garden. During the Yuan Dynasty, the "Wanjuan Building" ("Ten Thousand Volumes Building") was constructed. During the Ming Dynasty, the "Zhou School" was expanded to a "Prefecture School", and Two Cheng Academies[2], Jintai Academy and Shanggu Academy were also constructed. During the reign of Yongzheng of the Qing Dynasty, the Lotus Pond Academy was established. The excellent historical and cultural heritage has produced a large number of historical celebrities: Guo Kui (a minister of the Yan State during the Spring and Autumn Period and the Warring States Period), Jing Ke (a righteous hero), Liu Bei (Emperor Zhaolie of the Han Dynasty), Zhao Kuangyin (Song Taizu), scientists such as Zu Chongzhi and Li Daoyuan, and Yuan Drama masters such as Guan Hanqing, Wang Shipu, etc., were all born on this land. Baoding is the birthplace of the Work-Study Movement in France, which has cultivated a large number of early Chinese revolutionaries such as Cai Hesen, Zhao Shiyan, Zhou Enlai, Li Weihan, Li Fuchun, Deng Xiaoping, Chen Yi, Nie Rongzhen, Cai Chang, and Xiang Jingyu. The first modern army officer school in the late Qing Dynasty was built in the eastern suburbs of Baoding, where senior generals such as Ye Ting, Zhao Bosheng, and Kuomintang generals such as Chiang Kai-shek, Bai Chongxi, Chen Cheng, Gu Zhutong, and Liu Zhi once studied.

Baoding was also an important area for the Boxer Rebellion activities, the birthplace of the Xinhai Revolution in North China, and the birthplace of the first Communist Party branch in Hebei. The surging anti-imperialist, anti-feudal, anti-Japanese struggles and the Civil War (1946—1949) led by the Communist Party of China have all left glorious achievements here. Works such as *Keep the Red Flag Flying, Wind and Cloud in the Early Days of That War, Zhang Ga the Soldier Boy,* and *Struggles in an Ancient City* all record the brilliance of Baoding's past.

---

[1] Zhou, a term of administrative division in ancient China.
[2] "Two Cheng" refers to Cheng Hao and Cheng Yi. Both are the important founders of the Neo-Confucianism in the Northern Song Dynasty.

Chapter 14
Zhengding

—A Thousand-Year-Old County in the Modern Times

Coming to Zhengding, one can see the ancient and majestic city wall, which looks like an elder dressed in formal attire, standing proudly while going through the test of time, and writing swiftly about the thrilling past of the thousand-year-old city's prosperity, collapse, and rebirth. The ancient city wall is a grand masterpiece of Zhengding's rich and colorful history. Despite having experienced wars, fires, and the erosion of time, the collapsed and ruined city wall now

Night view of Zhengding Ancient City
正定古城夜景

has been rebuilt and is exuding a new charm. Along the city wall above the city gate, stands the "Wangchenglou", a tall tower that enables one to take an overall view of the whole city. With its gable and hip roof[①] and the upturned eaves, the tower looks magnificent. On the city wall beneath the tower, there is a tablet with four bold characters of " 三关雄镇 " ("A Mighty Town Connecting Three Passes") hanging high up above the city's gate. Climbing up to the top of the city wall and gazing far into the distance, one can overlook the ancient city with lofty pagodas, tranquil temples, and magnificent buildings dating from various dynasties including Tang, Song, Yuan, Ming, and Qing dynasties, which constitute the amazing skyline of Zhengding. By the sparkling moat river are the busy streets, and the prosperity reflected in the verse "the city is brilliantly illuminated, with music drifting from people's homes" seems also back in front of people's eyes. What's more, the city becomes even more gorgeous when the night falls, as its pagodas glitter like colored glaze, towering into the sky among the "sea" of lights. Those pagodas, including the Xumi Pagoda of the Tang Dynasty, the Lingxiao Pagoda of the Song Dynasty, the grand, ingeniously constructed Hua Pagoda, and the exquisite Chengling Pagoda—which seem to be crystal clear when brightly lit—emit and reflect light from people's homes, combining elegance with secularity, as well as antiquity with modernity. In the gourmet streets where red lanterns glow, aromatic smells waft up from the bustling marketplace. Indeed, the ancient city is humming with life. Just as the old saying goes, "One can always climb up the high towers, see the ancient pagodas, and rekindle those nostalgic memories." As you take a bird's eye view of the a-thousand-year-old city, you might be touched and meditate on the past of the city.

With the Taihang Mountains to its west and the Hutuo River to its south, Zhengding's advantageous geographical location always made it a battleground for strategists and a place where different ethnic groups converged and integrated. Due to the blending and coexistence of various ethnic groups, it became the most prosperous metropolis on the North China Plain. During the Song Dynasty, it was a mixed settlement of ethnic minorities such as the Khitan, Jurchen, and Mongols, as well as the Han

---

① gable and hip roof : also known as a hipped roof, one of the ancient Chinese architectural roof styles.

people, where ethnic integration and economic and cultural development took place. During the Yuan Dynasty, the commodity economy flourished, attracting many travelling Arab merchants as well as merchants from the Western Regions and other places.

The profound cultural accumulation has nourished this land, and the Hutuo River, which has been flowing for thousands of years, has given birth to the tenacious and upright cultural spirit of Zhengding. The people of Zhengding have always valued sincerity and righteousness since ancient times. Many historical figures have embraced the great virtues of patriotism and benevolence, prioritizing the interests of the nation and the state. For example, during the Qin and Han Dynasties, the famous statesman and military strategist Zhao Tuo was ordered to conquer Lingnan[①]. He adopted the policy of "pacifying and integrating the local ethnic minorities" and promoting national unity, and was the earliest patriotic pioneer to spread the Central Plains culture and advanced production methods to Lingnan. The famous general Zhao Zilong (Zhao Yun) of the Three Kingdoms Period, a native of Zhengding, Changshan Prefecture (today's Zhengding), served as a model of ancient loyal ministers and good generals, and a perfect embodiment of both wisdom and courage. Zhao Yun's "perfect hero" image has deeply embedded in people's hearts, becoming an outstanding representative of Zhengding's cultural spirit.

The long-standing history has left numerous diverse cultural relics and splendid local cultural heritages in the ancient city of Zhengding. It had been an important part of the Zhongshan State, the Hengshan Prefecture, and the Changshan Prefecture in ancient Chinese history. It has a large number of architectural relics left from the ancient times, which are distinctive in terms of style. For example, there are nine ancient bridges[②], nine towers, four pagodas, eight temples and twenty-four golden archways. Due to historical changes, many precious relics have been destroyed,

---

① "Lingnan" refers to the region south of the Five Ridges, which includes the areas of today's Guangdong Province and Guangxi Province.

② What is unique about these bridges is each bridge has three roads, and there is no river under them. In ancient times, the main purpose of these bridges was not to solve the traffic problems, but to serve as a symbol of Chinese ancient ritual system.

Yanghe Tower
九楼之首——阳和楼

but the four pagodas of Lingxiao Pagoda, Hua Pagoda, Sumeru Pagoda, and Chengling Pagoda, as well as the eight temples including Longxing Temple, Guanghui Temple, Linji Temple, Kaiyuan Temple, and Tianning Temple, still remain. Along with the legends of the temples and the stories of the pagodas, the extraordinary experiences and legends of historical celebrities constitute the cornerstone of Zhengding's rich culture. In 1993, Zhengding was approved by the State Council as a national historical and cultural city.

Entering from the Changle Gate at the south of the ancient city and climbing up the ancient city wall, you can see the four pagodas of Lingxiao Pagoda, Hua Pagoda, Sumeru Pagoda, and Chengling Pagoda standing and echoing each other.

The Hua Pagoda of Guanghui Temple, also known as the Flower Pagoda, has various intricate floral decorations on the upper half of its body, looking like a blooming bouquet from a distance. The Hua Pagoda was originally built during the Tang Dynasty, and what we see now is the remain of the reconstruction during the Dading Period (1161—1189 AD) of the Jin Dynasty. This type of pagoda almost disappeared after the Yuan Dynasty, and there are only about a dozen such pagodas existing in China.

Its artistic value and important position in Chinese architectural history have been praised by the famous Chinese architect Mr. Liang Sicheng as a "unique example within the country". It is worth noting that there are interesting sculptures on the pagoda body, including elephants, tigers, and Buddha images, all vividly portrayed.

Longxing Temple is located on the north side of Zhongshan East Road in Zhengding County, covering an area of 60,000 square meters. It is one of the largest ancient architectural complexes in Hebei Province. There are six cultural relics in the temple that can be regarded as the best in the country: the Manichaean Hall of the Song Dynasty, which boasts a distinctive style and was praised by the master of ancient architecture Mr. Liang Sicheng as a unique example of world ancient architecture; the colorful hanging sculpture of Guanyin Bodhisattva, which was praised as the "God of Oriental Beauty" by Mr. Lu Xun; the largest early rotary sutra repository in China; the Longzang Temple Stele, known as "the best stele

Oriental God of Beauty in Longxing Temple
隆兴寺摩尼殿中的倒坐观音

of the Sui Dynasty" and the "ancestor of regular script"; the 21.3-meter-high bronze-cast Thousand-Hand Thousand-Eye Guanyin Bodhisattva, which is the tallest ancient bronze Buddha in China; and the ingeniously designed, rich in variation, and exquisitely crafted bronze-cast sculpture of Thousand Buddhas Supporting and Surrounding the Vairocana Buddha, which is considered a unique treasure in China. At the same time, the temple also gathers various treasures such as inscriptions, murals, and porcelains from past dynasties, all of which have high historical, artistic, and scientific value. The master of ancient architecture, Mr. Liang Sicheng, once praised, "Among the famous temples outside Beijing, Longxing Temple in Zhengding is the best."

Linji Temple is the ancestral temple of the Linji Sect, one of the five schools of Chan Buddhism. Unfortunately, the buildings of Linji Temple were destroyed in the wars during the Song and Jin Dynasties, and only the Chengling Pagoda has been preserved. The Chengling Pagoda is an octagonal nine-story solid brick multi-eaved pagoda, featuring a distinct Liao and Jin pagoda style. The pagoda is 30.47 meters high, with the first storey being taller and the height of each storey decreasing from the second level upwards. The pagoda's top has wooden eave corner beams, with bells hanging under the eaves. The pagoda's top, the eave tiles, the ridge beasts, and the set beasts are all made of green glazed tiles, so it is also called the Green Pagoda. The Linji Sect was introduced to Japan during the Jin Dynasty and had a profound influence on it. To this day, many Japanese monks still come here to pay their respects.

Chapter 15
Shanhaiguan Pass

—The First Pass under Heaven

Shanhaiguan Pass is a national historical and cultural city, a world cultural heritage site, a national key cultural relics protection unit, and a national 5A-level tourist attraction. It is the most complete ancient military defense system preserved in China to date and serves as "the natural Great Wall museum".

Shanhaiguan Pass, also known as "Yuguan Pass" in ancient times, is located 15 kilometers northeast of Qinhuangdao City, Hebei Province. It is one of the northeastern passes of the Great Wall of the Ming Dynasty, and one of the "three wonders of the Great Wall" (namely, Shanhaiguan Pass in the east, Zhenbeitai Fortress in the middle, and Jiayuguan Pass in the

west). It is known as "the First Pass under Heaven" and "the unparalleled strategic gateway of Shenyang and Beijing, and the first pass of the ten-thousand-mile Great Wall", echoing the famous Jiayuguan Pass tens and thousands of miles away. It is located at the foot of the Yanshan Mountains on the north, the Bohai Sea on the south, bordering Suizhong County of Liaoning on the northeast, and connected to Funing District of Qinghuangdao City of Hebei on the northwest. Situated between the Jiaoshan Mountain and the Bohai Sea, it has beautiful scenery integrating mountain, sea, pass, river, and lake landscapes. As the saying goes, "It is the first pass to the east of Beijing, which is connected to the sea and pillowing the green mountain." The "green mountain" mentioned here refers to the first mountain that the Great Wall of the early Ming Dynasty crossed—the Jiaoshan Mountain, which has a dangerous terrain, easy to defend and difficult to attack, and serves as a natural barrier for Shanhaiguan Pass. The Old Dragon's Head ("Laolongtou" in Chinese) is the only section of the Great Wall that extends into the sea, and it is the most unique part of the Great Wall. The distance between the mountain and the sea in Shanhaiguan Pass is only 8 kilometers. The Great Wall, like a giant dragon, winds its way westward among the mountains, connecting the high mountains, the majestic passes, and the vast sea, forming the unique geography of the Shanhaiguan Pass.

As the eastern starting point of the Great Wall, Shanhaiguan Pass controls the Liaoxi Corridor. The majestic Great Wall follows the ups and downs of the mountains, with dense watchtowers, dominating the surrounding area.

In the fourteenth year of the Hongwu reign of the Ming Dynasty (1381), General Xu Da dispatched 15,100 soldiers from the Yanshan Garrison and other places to build thirty-two passes in Yongping, Jieling, and other areas. In December of that year, the Shanhaiwei City was built, which is the origin of the name Shanhaiguan Pass. Since then, Shanhaiguan Pass has become an important pass for controlling the Liaodong Peninsula.

The current Shanhaiguan Pass has well preserved the historical features of the Ming and Qing dynasties. Its defensive architecture layout fully utilized the topographical features of the Shanhaiguan area and was designed according to the method of "adapting to the terrain and using the fortresses to defend the border". Shanhaiguan Pass had built a unique defense system consisting of the main city, the urn cities (an urn city is also known as a "Wengcheng" in Chinese), two semicircular protective cities ("Dongluocheng" and "Xiluocheng"), two wing cities (the South Wing City and the North Wing City), outpost castles, coastal defense castles, and the Great Wall on the 8-kilometer-long narrow passage between the mountain and the sea. Having both land and sea defense facilities, as well as internal and external settings, and an in-depth three-dimensional defense system, the design of Shanhaiguan Pass fully demonstrates the ingenuity of Chinese people at that time.

In general, the defense system of Shanhaiguan Pass can be divided into two layers: inner and outer. The inner layer is centered on the main city, supplemented by the urn cities and and the two semicircular protective cities; the outer layer mainly consists of scattered outposts, wing cities, and various passes and beacon towers, forming a mutually

Old Dragon Head
老龙头

supporting relationship with the internal defense system.

The eastern wall of the main city of Shanhaiguan Pass is part of the Great Wall, while its southern, northern, and western walls surround the Great Wall. The entire city has a circumference of 4,796 meters, with walls 11.6 meters high and 10 meters thick. The inner part of the walls is filled with earth, while the outer part is covered with bricks. In the regions east of Beijing, the main city of Shanhaiguan Pass is the largest and the most solidly-built one among its counterparts. There is a city gate in the middle of each of the four walls: the east gate is called Zhendong Gate, the west gate is Ying'en Gate, the south gate is Wangyang Gate, and the north gate is Weiyuan Gate. Each city gate has a gate tower, and there are five gate towers on the eastern wall, namely Zhendong Tower, Jingbian Tower, Muying Tower, Linlü Tower, and Weijin Hall, collectively known as the "Five Tigers Guarding the East". Outside the city gates are urn cities. In the twelfth year of the Wanli reign of the Ming Dynasty (1584), the eastern semicircular protective city was built outside the east gate, and in the sixteenth year of the Chongzhen reign of the Ming Dynasty (1643), the western semicircular protective city was built outside the west gate, ultimately forming the defense system seen today.

The outer defensive facilities that are currently preserved and relatively intact include Ninghai City and Zhenlu Platform, while the remaining South Wing City, North Wing City, and Weiyuan City only have some remnants, with the main buildings no longer in existence. Within the jurisdiction of Shanhaiguan Pass, from the Old Dragon's Head on the shore of the Bohai Sea in the south to the Jiumenkou in the depths of the Yanshan Mountains in the north, along the 26-kilometer-long Great Wall, there are ten key passes set up in strategically important locations: Nanhaikou Pass, Nanshui Pass, Shanhaiguan Pass, Beishui Pass, Hanmen Pass, Jiaoshan Pass, Lanshui Pass, Sandao Pass, Si'eryu Pass, and Yipianshi Pass. In addition, there are 43 watchtowers, 51 gate tower platforms, and 14 beacon towers, which together form the in-dept defense system of Shanhaiguan Pass. The defense system is strictly guarded, mutually supportive, and well-structured, with clear functions and flexible offense and defense capabilities. It can be considered a masterpiece of ancient military defense systems.

As a military stronghold, Shanhaiguan Pass is an important transportation hub and serves as a political, cultural, and economic transit center between the inner and outer regions. The main city, as the core of the ancient city complex, has formed a unique urban layout within. This military-oriented city is structured around the north-south and east-west main streets, with alleys, lanes, residential houses, shops, temples, ancestral halls, and government offices distributed throughout the city. The area is culturally developed, commercially prosperous, and bustling with people, showing vitality and vigor everywhere. The harmonious unity of its spatial organization and three-dimensional contours reflects the artistic achievements of ancient Chinese urban architecture. Despite the turmoil of wars, the layout of the Ming and Qing dynasties has been relatively well preserved, making it a model for studying the layout of ancient cities.

In conclusion, Shanhaiguan Pass not only leaves people with an ancient military fortress that has experienced countless battles and the test of time, but also a historic city with profound cultural heritage. It is a testament to civilization and progress, and an enduring monument in the history of culture.

◈ Chapter 16
Handan

—A City with a History of 3,000 Years

The name "Handan" has remained unchanged as a unique city name for approximately 3,000 years.

The ancient city of Handan, located at the southern end of Hebei Province, is bordered by the Taihang Mountains to the west and the North China Plain in the east. It is adjacent to the three provinces of Shanxi, Shandong, and Henan. Handan is a national historical and cultural city and is known as the "capital of Chinese idioms and allusions".

In 1965, a large number of alliance documents from the late Spring and Autumn Period, made of jade discs or jade tablets, were unearthed in Houma County (today's Houma City, a county-level city), Shanxi Province. The name "Handan" appeared many times in these documents, indicating that the name of "Handan" was established no later than the Spring and Autumn Period. As a city name, "Handan" has remained unchanged for about three thousand

Wuling Congtai in Handan
邯郸 武灵丛台

years, making it unique in China.

Handan is a national historical and cultural city, with 115 national and provincial cultural relics protection units and more than 1,500 cultural relics protection sites, scattered like pearls at the foot of the lush Purple Mountain and beside the gurgling Fuyang River. The grain crops unearthed from Cishan revealed the origin of human agricultural civilization; Zhao Wangcheng (the palace of ancient Zhao State), covered in the dust of time, has become the most best-preserved royal city of the Warring States Period; the majestic and lofty Wuling Congtai Terrace still retains its charm; Golden Millet Dream Temple, an ancient Taoist architecture, implies the ancient people's reflection on life; the Bronze Sparrow Terrace demonstrates the vigor of the Wei State in the Three Kingdoms Period; Huiche Alley records the everlasting story of "the reconciliation between the General Lian Po and the Minister Lin Xiangru"; Wa Huang Palace combines myths and legends with a "dynamic and static" temple on the cliff side[1]; in Xiangtangshan Grottoes, Buddhist art has been intricately carved into each grotto. As you take a walk along the streets with their stone and pottery walls in Pengcheng town, you will gasp in admiration for the thousand-year craft of Cizhou kiln that has been passed on generation after generation; when you listen to the story of the Xuebu Bridge[2], you will be amused by both the mockery for those rigid imitators and the derision for those who completely dance to predecessor's tune; as you visit the tombs of the Northern Dynasties, which are among wild flowers and green grass now, the melody of *Prince Lanling Entering the Battlefield* seems to

Cishan Culture
磁山文化

① This temple is "shaky". It has no solid foundation, but is bound to the steep cliff by nine strong iron chains! If too many people climb up the building, it will lean slightly forward, so it is also called a "living building" or a "hung temple".
② Xuebu Bridge, also known as "the Learning Walking Bridge," implies the story of a young man who came to Handan to learn how to walk gracefully, but finally failed and even forgot how to walk in his own way.

be echoing in your ears.

As early as 8,000 years ago, there were human beings living and reproducing here, giving birth to the early Neolithic Cishan Culture. The Cishan Culture predates the Yangshao Culture and Longshan Culture by more than 2,000 years. According to the investigations by the Institute of Archaeology of the Chinese Academy of Social Sciences, the Cishan Culture dates back more than 7,300 years, advancing China's Neolithic era by more than 1,000 years. During the Warring States Period, Handan served as the capital of the Zhao State for 158 years and was the political, economic, and cultural center of northern China. The culture of Zhao State, represented by "Wearing the Hu Attire and Shooting from Horseback", embodies the main values of "pioneering spirit, competition consciousness, and inclusiveness", reflecting the spirit of reform and innovation of Zhao State during its pursuit of power in the Central Plains. The culture is the crystallization of the convergence, integration, and sublimation of the Chinese Central Plains culture and the northern grassland nomadic culture, possessing the characteristic of duality and reflecting the process of conflict and integration among various ethnic groups in northern China. After the unification of China by the Qin State, Handan became one of the 36 prefectures of the Qin Dynasty, with the ancient Handan city as its political center. During the Han Dynasty, Handan shared the title of "the Five Great Capitals" with Chang'an, Luoyang, Linzi, and Chengdu. At the end of the Eastern Han Dynasty, Cao Cao established the capital in the area around Yecheng, a city in the southern part of Handan. During the Northern Song Dynasty, Daming, which is in the eastern part of Handan, became the auxiliary capital of the country, along with the capital Bianliang (today's Kaifeng). Shexian County of Handan was the location of the 129th Division Command of the Eighth Route Army and the Jin-Ji-Lu-Yu Border Region Government (or Shanxi-Hebei-Shandong-Henan Border Region Government) during the War of Resistance against Japan and the China's War of Liberation. The "Taihang Horn", a group of wartime journalists, traversed the valleys and ridges of the Taihang Mountains, spreading the news about communist-led revolution throughout the mountains and rivers of North China. The "Man-made Milky Way", Yuefeng Canal, was built on the cliffs, winding around the mountains and rushing through the peaks at an average altitude of 170 meters, bringing clear water from the Taihang Mountains.

Cizhou kiln is one of the birthplaces of pottery production in China, and its influence extends to the provinces of Shanxi, Hebei, Shandong, Henan, Shaanxi, and several southern provinces. Cizhou kiln has a long history; during the Cishan Culture period, the ancestors in this area had already produced exquisite pottery. Subsequently, painted pottery was produced during the Yangshao Culture period, black pottery was produced in the Longshan Culture period, and gray pottery was produced in the Shang Dynasty. Eventually celadon and cosmetic white porcelain (Due to the relatively poor quality of the porcelain clay used in Cizhou kiln, porcelain bodies are usually gray or grayish-brown, making it difficult to produce decent white porcelain. To compensate for this defect, Cizhou kiln potters used a white cosmetic clay to cover porcelain bodies, giving birth to the cosmetic white porcelain) were made in the Northern Dynasties and the Sui Dynasty, realizing the transition from pottery to porcelain.

Handan culture is one of the sources of the ancient Chinese culture and an important pillar of the Central Plains culture. It is rich, profound, dazzling, well-known, and charming. This is a place where you can grasp a handful of soil and squeeze out the essence of ancient civilizations!

Today's Handan is changing rapidly. Relying on the sites and

Handan East Ring and Renmin Road Interchange
邯郸市东环与人民路立交桥

heritage related to the CPC and the rich ecological resources of the Taihang Mountains, Handan is accelerating the construction of the Taihang Red River Valley Cultural Tourism Economic Belt with the image positioning of "Heroic Taihang Mountains, China's Red River Valley", striving to build the national research and tourism demonstration zone of the revolutionary traditions and heritages, the Taihang green industry demonstration zone, and the characteristic landscape tourism destination. In addition, the dryland terraces in Shexian County are built on a grand scale, with countless pieces of rocks as the bases. Looking down from the air, you can see intersecting gullies and ridges, as well as towering mountains, along which rows upon rows of terraced fields stretching boundlessly beyond your view, going all the way towards the top of the mountains. It looks like the mountains have lifted layers of delicate waves, arranged in rows, layer upon layer, reaching the summit, forming a magnificent and unique terrace landscape.

Looking back, you may find that the past has never been forgotten, but written in the glorious annals of history; looking forward, Handan still has a long way to go. The future is calling on its people to draw up a new blueprint, and Handan, this historical and cultural city, is now standing at a new starting point in history with a new image.

Chapter 17
Yuxian County

— "The Ancient Architecture Museum" of Hebei

At the foot of the Taihang Mountains, the past of an ancient royal city has been sealed off by dust. Layers upon layers of tile-ends are recounting the former magnificence of the palaces, and the broken walls are telling the stories about the bygone glory of the city. The Taihang Eight Passes, including the Feihu Valley Pass, have not only survived the war-ridden times, but

Nuanquan Ancient Town
暖泉古镇

also seen the coming and going of countless trade caravans. The ancient Yuzhou, one of the sixteen prefectures in ancient northern China, has turned into today's Yuxian County with its vibrant culture after more than a thousand years of time. In Yuxian County, there are eight hundred castles for village protection and eight hundred theaters for plays and performances, which demonstrate the richness of the county's history. Here, people's life stories can be engraved into paper-cutting, and their happiness and hope for future can be expressed in a ladle of molten iron poured on walls, which strikes a shower of sparks like canopies and flowers. The colorful cultural heritages passed on from generation to generation are still being displayed in today's Yuxian County.

There are two ancient cities in today's Yuxian County: Daiwangcheng (the royal city of ancient Dai State) and Yuzhou Ancient City. Both of them have a long history, with Daiwangcheng standing at the beginning of the history of this land. Daiwangcheng is about 10 kilometers east of the county town. After about 3,000 years, it still can be seen today that the city wall of Daiwangcheng takes on an oval shape, with a circumference of nearly 10 kilometers, which is rare in ancient city walls. The city wall is well-preserved, with nine city gates such as Xinglong Gate and Baoyuan Gate, etc. The cultural heritage of Yuxian County, therefore, is abundant.

Yuzhou Ancient City is 10 kilometers away from Daiwangcheng and has a circumference of more than 3,800 meters, with a history of more than 1,400 years. Yuzhou Ancient City had challenged the traditional rules of city construction, taking on an irregular shape instead of the traditional square shape. Its buildings are asymmetry. There is a moat outside the ancient city, and a suspension bridge connects it to the inner city.

Feihu Ancient Route, also known as Feihu Pass, is an extremely dangerous passage among the eight passes of the Taihang Mountains. It winds for 35 kilometers in Yuxian County. During the Ming and Qing Dynasties, mule and horse caravans and camel caravans from the Central Plains region carried goods along the Feihu Ancient Route, making the route an important commercial artery, and also bringing prosperity to Yuxian County. What's more, this ancient route was not only a trading route, but also a route of strategic importance in wars. Yuxian County is located at the throat of Feihu Ancient Route, becoming a vital transportation hub connecting the North China Plain and the desert outside the Great Wall. Yuxian County became a prosperous commercial center at that time due to the Feihu Ancient Route. For thousands of years, Yuxian County has gathered merchants from all over the world, rendering it a place with diverse cultures and ingenious ancient architectures. History has left its marks on the bricks and tiles here, and the developing process of Yuxian County has been recorded by these ancient architectures.

The long history has left a large number of amazing cultural landscapes in Yuxian County. The county town of Yuxian County was first built in the second year of the Daxiang reign of the Northern Zhou Dynasty (580 AD) and was renovated in the tenth year of the Hongwu reign of the Ming Dynasty (1377 AD). It is the most well-preserved ancient town to the west of Beijing. Yuxian County now has more than 1,610 cultural relics sites, among which more than 20 are national-level cultural relics protection units, making it the county with the most national-level protected cultural relics in China. The Jade Emperor Pavilion, Nan'an Temple Pagoda, and Shakyamuni Temple in the county town are all national key cultural relic protection units. These ancient architectural complexes, with architectural styles from the Liao, Yuan, Ming, and Qing Dynasties, and reflecting the cultural characteristics of Confucianism,

Ancient City Wall of YuZhou

蔚州城墙

Buddhism, and Taoism, together with the Daiwangcheng ruins close to the county town, the rare Chongtai Temple integrating the three cultures of Confucianism, Buddhism, and Taoism, and the ancient castles, temples, residences, and theater buildings scattered around, have withstood the wind and rain for more than a thousand years. They constitute the extremely rich historical and cultural heritage of Yuxian County and have earned it the reputation of "the ancient architecture museum".

As the saying goes, "In the south, there are Fujian Tulou[①], while in the north, there are ancient castles of Yuxian County." The ancient buildings represented by the castles in Yuxian County not only share the common features of traditional Han Chinese architecture in the Central Plains region but also have their unique strategic defensive characteristics as a part of the strategic defense system complementing the Great Wall. As the epitome of Yuxian County, the layout of the castles and streets in Ancient Nuanquan Town is still well preserved today. There are numerous ancient buildings such as pavilions, terraces, and towers, with a rigorous layout and an orderly arrangement of heights and sizes, reflecting the influence of traditional Chinese culture on architecture and the ancient construction principles passed down through generations. In Yuxian County, it is said that there are 800 castles for village protection and 800 theaters for plays and performances; in every village, there are old theaters, each with its unique form.

Ancient buildings are not only landmarks of Yuxian County but also bridges connecting the past and present. They have witnessed the changes of this land from Yuzhou to Yuxian County. These buildings are like old photos that record the past glory and prosperity of this land.

---

① Tulou, the unique residential architectures in Fujian Province.

 Exercises

Ⅰ. Comprehension

（1）In which city is the Governor-general's Mansion of Zhili of the Qing Dynasty located, and how did this city get its name?

（2）In which city in Hebei are there the most Tang and Song Dynasty-style wooden buildings? Which famous general from the Three Kingdoms Period was born there?

（3）Which two cities in Hebei are respectively known as "The Number One City of Yan-Zhao" and "The Number One Zhou in China"?

（4）In addition to the national historical and cultural cities mentioned in this part, there are many ancient counties in Hebei that have a history of over a thousands years. Try to find out more about these ancient counties.

Ⅱ. Translation

1. Term Translation

（1）春蒐、夏苗、秋狝、冬狩

（2）三关雄镇

（3）涟漪夏艳

（4）代蔚长歌

2. Passage Translation

承德位于长城北侧，是农耕文明和游牧文明的过渡地带。因特殊的地理位置被清朝选中，夏季避暑，冬季为北京阻挡严寒，还是怀柔四方的舞台，开启了承德历史上最为高光的时期。很少有像承德这种从兴起、繁荣到衰落均在一个朝代完成的城市。

Part Four

Intangible Cultural Heritages Nurtured in This Fragrant Land

The long history and splendid civilization of Hebei have nurtured a rich and diverse variety of folk arts with various forms.

As of June 10, 2021, Hebei Province had 163 national intangible cultural heritage items, among which Yuxian County Paper-cutting, Fengning Manchu Paper-cutting, Tangshan Shadow Puppetry, Yang-style Tai Chi, Wu-style Tai Chi, and Wang Qihe Tai Chi have been included in the UNESCO Representative List of the Intangible Cultural Heritage of Humanity.

Hebei's local folk arts, such as local operas, Quyi[①], characteristic handicrafts, ancient folk music, folk fine arts, Cangzhou martial arts, and Wuqiao acrobatics, enjoy a high reputation both at home and abroad. These arts reflect the cultural traditions of the Chinese nation from different perspectives, and their common feature is that they originate from folk life. Some are inherited from history, some are transplanted from other provinces, and some are created in new forms. Eventually, they gradually form a strong local flavor and are deeply loved by the masses.

In the long course of historical development, Hebei's folk arts have played an intangible role in cultivating people's sentiments, entertaining their minds and bodies, expressing emotions, and exchanging ideas.

---

① Quyi is the general term for various "narrative and singing arts" of the Chinese nation. It is a unique art form formed through the long-term development and evolution of folk oral literature and singing arts, including ballad singing, story telling, comic dialogues, clapper talks, cross talks, etc.

Lead-in Questions

(1) Intangible cultural heritage is an important symbol of a country's and a nation's historical and cultural achievements and an essential part of excellent traditional culture. What do you know about China's intangible cultural heritage?

(2) How is Chinese intangible cultural heritage classified, and can you give some examples that we come across in our daily lives?

(3) In Hebei's intangible cultural heritage, which ones are national-level intangible cultural heritage?

(4) Before reading this division, have you ever met or learned about any intangible cultural heritage inheritor?

Hebei National Intangible Cultural Heritage—Yishui inkstone

河北省国家级非物质文化遗产——易水砚

Chapter 18
Yuxian County Paper-Cutting
—The Soulful Flowers Blooming on this Ancient Land

Yuxian County Paper-cutting
蔚县剪纸

Yuxian County Paper-cutting is a unique folk art in Hebei Province, with a history of more than 200 years. Its production process stands out among numerous paper-cutting styles in China. Yuxian County paper-cutting is the only dyeing paper-cutting in China that mainly uses intaglio and supplements it with relief, placing great emphasis on both carving and dyeing. It is made from thin Xuan paper[①], carved with a small and sharp carving knife, and then dyed with bright and brilliant colors. The basic production process includes: designing patterns, creating templates, carving, and dyeing. On May 20, 2006, Yuxian County Paper-cutting was approved by the State Council to be included in the first batch of the National Intangible Cultural Heritage List.

Yuxian County Paper-cutting is best known for its window decorations. "Tianpiliang" can be considered the earliest form of window decoration, which involves painting and coloring on thin mica sheets for decoration. In the early days, the use of "patterns" for embroidering on shoes, sachets, and pillows also popularized in this area. Later, the woodblock watermark window decorations from Wuqiang County, Hebei, were introduced. Yuxian County Paper-cutting absorbed its color

---

① Xuan paper, a high quality paper made in Xuancheng, Anhui Province. It is often used for traditional Chinese painting and calligraphy.

characteristics and imitated the transparent effect of "Tianpiliang". By using carving instead of cutting, a unique style of Yuxian County Paper-cutting was formed.

Yuxian County Paper-cutting is rich and diverse in its types, including not only depictions of opera characters, birds, insects, fish, and beasts, but also detailed portrayals of rural life. These paper-cutting works, whether reflecting people's hopes for auspiciousness and happiness, or celebrating seasonal festivals, weddings, and birthdays, whether drawing inspirations from popular historical stories and folk legends popular among the people, or representing the unique cultural background and folk customs of the north, all demonstrate the superb wisdom and rich imagination of folk artists. These works are full and rich in composition, vivid in shape, being rustic and exquisite, delicate and simple, and having a strong sense of life and profound meanings. Together with well-arranged design, meticulous and exquisite carving skills, and brilliant and unique coloring, each piece is vivid and appealing, and possesses practical value, ornamental value, as well as collectible value. When pasted on window papers and illuminated by outdoor light, they appear exceptionally exquisite, transparent, colorful, and lively, exuding a cheerful, bright, and refreshing charm.

Throughout the long years of continuous development of Yuxian County Paper-cutting, not only have a large number of increasingly excellent works been created, but many outstanding paper-cutting artists have also been cultivated. Wang Laoshang (1890—1951), a native of Nan Zhangzhuang Village in Yuxian County, is an outstanding representative among them. He was particularly skilled at depicting distinctive characters in operas, such as Sheng, Dan, Jing, Mo, and Chou[1], and created a large number of works that were deeply loved by the masses. Before Wang Laoshang, although Yuxian County Paper-cutting had a long history, its carving was rough, the images of the characters were rigid, and there were only a limited number of colors used in the dyeing process. After his reform, the window decorations and various opera characters he carved broke away from the past monotonous, identical, and rigid appearance. His carving skills were refined, the patterns were elegant, the expressions were

① Sheng, Dan, Jing, Mo, and Chou are categories of character roles in Beijing Opera.

vivid and lifelike, and the characters had distinct personalities, which were well-received by the masses.

After the successful bid for the Beijing Winter Olympics, the paper-cutting artists of Yuxian County began to create paper-cutting works with the Winter Olympics as the theme. During the closing ceremony of the 2018 Pyeongchang Winter Olympics, the "Beijing 8 Minutes" performance was brilliantly staged. In the documentary broadcasted at the same time, there was a seven-meter-long paper-cutting scroll created by the artists of Yuxian County, which was created specifically for the Winter Olympics. Winter Olympic elements have injected a new life into the art of paper-cutting. Thanks to the Winter Olympics, Yuxian County Paper-cutting has become more widely known to people around the world, and this intangible cultural heritage art continues to develop through inheritance and innovation.

Chapter 19

Hengshui Interior Painting

—Miraculous Craftsmanship Inside a Small Bottle

The art of interior painting is a unique traditional art form in China. By taking glass, crystal, amber, and other materials as the bottle base, and using a specially made deformed fine brush, exquisite patterns, including figures, landscapes, flowers, birds, and calligraphy, can be painted or written inside the bottles, with an elegant style, exquisite brushwork, and brilliant colors, which demonstrates infinite imagination and creativity within a small space.

Hengshui Interior Painting
衡水内画

In the 17th century, snuff became popular in Europe and was introduced to China during the late Ming and early Qing Dynasties. At that time, the main container was snuffboxes, which later evolved into unique Chinese-style snuff bottles. Nowadays, the habit of using snuff has almost disappeared, but snuff bottles have been passed down as exquisite and pocket-sized art pieces, mainly due to the art of interior painting. The production of interior painted snuff bottles includes a series of processes such as material selection, process production, and decoration. The materials cover six major categories: metal, jade, stone, pottery, glass, and organic materials. The craftsmanship involves traditional techniques such as writing, drawing, carving, and engraving, etc. Snuff bottles became a miniature representation of the Qing Dynasty's arts and crafts, and were later hailed as "pocket-sized art pieces that incorporate a variety of Chinese craftsmanship", earning worldwide acclaim.

Interior painting is different from exterior painting in two ways. First, the painting order is reversed, and the interior painting needs to be done in a reversed order. Second, the painting angle is limited, as the artist can only paint through the bottle's opening, which restricts the operation due to its small size. It is also difficult to see the position of the brush

Hengshui Interior Painting
衡水内画

while painting, which greatly tests the artistic skills of the interior painting masters. When painting, artists need to concentrate and focus all their strength on their wrists. Most importantly, there is no room for error, as the painting must be completed in one attempt. Otherwise, even a tiny flaw may require the entire work to be redone from scratch.

The interior painting of snuff bottles is based on Chinese painting and inherits the essence of traditional Chinese art, featuring Chinese stories, landscapes, and culture, all vividly displayed within the small space of snuff bottles. Among them, the Beijing-style snuff bottles are the most well-known and have the longest history, followed by the development of distinctive schools such as Hebei-style, Shandong-style, and Guangdong-style. Beijing-style masters generally have a high level of literary and artistic cultivation, focusing on traditional themes and historical stories, using simple colors and rigorous structures, providing an elegant and unique artistic enjoyment. Hebei-style is known for its character portraits, capturing both form and spirit. In particular, interior painted works featuring children playing best reflect the artistic characteristics of Hebei-style interior painted snuff bottles. The most distinctive feature of Shandong-style is the ability to use glaze colors for painting on porcelain, and then firing to create interior painted snuff bottles with ceramic glaze paintings, which remain undamaged even when filled with water. Currently, the youngest school is the Guangdong-style, which is famous for its vibrant colors and decorative style.

Hengshui is the birthplace of Hebei-style interior painting, and due to its unique artistic style, it has been named the "Hometown of Chinese Interior Painting Art" by the Ministry of Culture. Wang Xisan, the founder of Hebei-style interior painting, was the first non-family disciple of Ye Xiaofeng and Ye Fengqi, who were the sons of the old Beijing-style artist Ye Zhongsan. In the late 1950s, after Wang Xisan had mastered the "Ye-style" interior painting techniques, he introduced the theme of depicting cats into the creation of interior painting. He used the meticulous "hair-tearing" method to paint vivid cat eyes and the fluffy texture of cat fur,

Hengshui Interior Painting
衡水内画

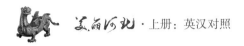
solving the problem of stiff and unrealistic cat images in traditional Chinese freehand painting. Wang Xisan created a special tool for Hebei-style interior painting, the metal-rod hook brush, also known as the "Xisan curved-hook brush". The brush handle is straight, but the brush tip is curved, allowing for easy changes in direction.

Hengshui interior painting, while inheriting the profound, simple, and elegant characteristics of Beijing-style, incorporates the delicate and smooth traditional painting techniques of Shandong-style. It also introduces traditional Chinese painting techniques into interior painting, which has greatly enriched the interior painting techniques. Later, oil painting was added to the interior painting, breaking the limitations of traditional single watercolor painting, and making the composition, image-depiction, and charm of interior painting reach a highly refined level, which has been hailed as a great feat of "combining Chinese and Western art". On May 20, 2006, Hengshui interior painting was included in the first batch of the National Intangible Cultural Heritage List.

🖼 Chapter 20
Anguo Medicinal Materials

—The Charm of the Millennium Medicine Capital

Anguo City, known as Qizhou in ancient times, is now under the jurisdiction of Baoding City in Hebei Province, and is 100 kilometers south of the provincial capital, Shijiazhuang. As early as over 700 years ago, during the Northern Song Dynasty, this place became a well-known distribution center for traditional Chinese medicinal materials in China. During the Daoguang reign of the Qing Dynasty, it reached its peak, and Qizhou was known as "The Capital for

Anguo Temple of the "King of Remedies"
安国药王庙

Medical Materials" and "The First Medical Material Market in the World", enjoying the great reputation of "Qizhou medicinal materials are famous worldwide".

The rise of Anguo medical material market originated from the construction of the Medicine King Temple (the Yaowang Temple). Located in the south of Anguo City (formerly the South Gate), this temple is the largest ancient architectural complex in China dedicated to commemorating medical sages throughout history. The Medicine King Temple was first built during the Eastern Han Dynasty, worshiping Pi Tong (whose courtesy name was Weijun), one of the twenty-eight generals of Liu Xiu, Emperor Guangwu of the Eastern Han Dynasty. During the Northern Song Dynasty, the Medicine King Temple was rebuilt on a new site, and people gathered to pay their homage to him. In the sixth year of Xianchun reign of the Southern Song Dynasty (1270), it was further honored as the "Mingling Zhaohui Xianwang". With the continuous bestowments from the emperors to Pi Tong, the influence of the "Medicine King" grew larger and larger. Since the establishment of the Medicine King Temple, people with illnesses have sought help from the Medicine King, and pious men and women often come to offer incense, making the temple very popular. Pharmaceutical merchants took advantage of this situation to sell medicine, gradually forming a medicine fair around the temple. By the middle of the Qing Dynasty, the "Thirteen Gangs" and the "Five Major Trade Associations" composed of pharmaceutical merchants from all over the country were formed, and the organization, called "Anke Hall" in Chinese, was established to accommodate and manage the market for merchants. Since then, Anguo has become the largest medicinal material exchange center and distribution center in northern China. From the Ming and Qing Dynasties to the Republic of China, the temple fair was organized in rotation by the "Thirteen Gangs". During the temple fair, the entire county was filled with the scent of medicine, making it very lively. The title of "Medicine Capital" have since become famous both domestically and internationally.

The Anguo Medicine King Temple Fair and the medicine market have a long history and a wide influence, occupying an important position in the history of the development of traditional Chinese medicine. As an economic and cultural carrier in the working mechanism of the society, the Medicine King Temple Fair has absorbed a vast amount of folk culture, embodying the thoughts, emotions, ideals, desires, moral customs, and aesthetic tastes of the local people and the majority of pharmaceutical merchants. It is not only the birthplace of Anguo's pharmaceutical industry but also directly nurtured the largest medicinal material distribution center in the country—the Anguo Medicine Market, playing an important role in promoting national medical exchanges and promoting Chinese medical culture. On May 20, 2006, the Anguo Medicine Market was approved by the State Council to be included in the first batch of National Intangible Cultural Heritage List.

In addition to the medicine market, Anguo's traditional Chinese medicine cultural industry also includes a Medicine Expo Park.

The Anguo Medicine Expo Park was built in 2016, with an 800-mu medicinal material planting landscape area, 300 kinds of traditional Chinese medicinal materials, a 1,000-mu demonstration area for authentic medicinal materials and the eight major Qizhou medicines, as well as a 200-mu intelligent greenhouse, a lavender manor, and a rapeseed flower garden. The park is an important guarantee for the construction of the Anguo Digital Chinese Medicine Capital project.

Established in 2005, the China Traditional Chinese Medicine Expo is the highest-level national exhibition in the traditional Chinese medicine industry, focusing on Chinese medicine pharmaceuticals, traditional Chinese medicine health products, Chinese medicinal materials (decoction pieces), traditional Chinese medicine pharmaceutical equipment, and international service trade in traditional Chinese medicine. Through a combination of exhibitions, transactions, and forums, it shares abundant promotional resources and marketing channels, striving to create a high-end platform for showcasing innovative achievements in traditional Chinese medicine and facilitating project negotiations.

In 2022, it was decided that the permanent venue for the China Traditional Chinese Medicine Expo will be located in Anguo City, Hebei Province.

Chapter 21
Shadow Puppetry

—A Myriad of Life Stories under the Light and Shadow

Shadow puppetry, also known as "shadow play" or "lamp-shadow play", is a type of puppet show popular in China, using character silhouettes made of animal hide or cardboard and performing behind a translucent cloth under the illumination of light. During the performance, artists manipulate the characters behind a white curtain while singing stories in local popular tunes, accompanied by percussion and string instruments, creating a strong local flavor. In the past, before the development of film and television media, shadow puppetry was one of the most popular folk entertainment activities. There are many schools of shadow puppetry, and Hebei is a major province for this art form. Currently, Tangshan shadow puppetry, Ji'nan shadow puppetry, and Hejian shadow puppetry from Hebei have been included in the National Intangible Cultural Heritage List.

Shadow Puppetry
皮影戏

Tangshan Shadow Puppetry

Hebei Tangshan shadow puppetry, also known as "Luanzhou shadow play", "Laoting shadow play", and "donkey-hide shadow play", is one of the most influential types of shadow puppetry in China. It is generally believed that Luanzhou shadow play was created in the late Ming Dynasty, flourished in the late Qing Dynasty and the early Republic of China, and has a history of more than 400 years. The characters and props are made of carved and colored donkey hide, so it is also called "donkey-hide shadow play". It is popular in Tangshan, Chengde, Langfang, and other regions of Hebei Province, as well as in cities and counties in the three northeastern provinces of China, and has a deep-rooted tradition among the masses. It is a popular art form among the local people. Tangshan shadow puppetry is a long-standing and far-reaching shadow puppetry school. The various shadow puppet singing styles in Hebei, Beijing, northeastern provinces, and Shandong regions all originated from Tangshan shadow puppetry. In 1966, Laoting County of Tangshan was named "The Hometown of Chinese Folk Art—The Hometown of Shadow Puppetry" by the Ministry of Culture.

Tangshan shadow puppetry is mainly based on historical stories, myths, and fables, with most of its themes coming from famous historical works. The themes are positive and uplifting, some depicting heroes who defend their homeland, some showcasing chivalrous figures who punish evil and promote good, and some portraying brave individuals who resist oppression. It celebrates truth, goodness, and beauty while denouncing falsehood, evil, and ugliness.

Tangshan shadow puppetry's repertoire is an important material for deeply analyzing the local society's customs, folkways, and religious psychology. Throughout the generations, Tangshan shadow puppet artists have never ceased to improve their techniques of singing performance and innovate the materials and craftsmanship of stage props. These experiences are invaluable treasures for both present and future generations. The inheritance of Tangshan shadow puppetry continues through the methods of oral teaching and heart-to-heart teaching, providing important reference value for cultural inheritance methods. Tangshan shadow puppetry's singing, music, performance, and modeling have a unique regional style, receiving praise from domestic and foreign peers and audiences, and possessing high appreciation and research value.

Ji'nan (southern Hebei) Shadow Puppetry

Ji'nan shadow puppetry is mainly popular in the southern part of Hebei, especially in the area centered around Feixiang District of Handan City, and it has influenced the central and northern parts of Hebei. Feixiang District is the birthplace of Ji'nan shadow puppetry, and the local people call it "cowhide shadow" "leather play" "poking leather play", or "one-eyed play". Feixiang shadow puppetry is based on traditional Chinese drama and appears in the style of folk paper-cutting, representing a typical example of Ji'nan shadow puppetry.

The character design of Ji'nan shadow puppetry is rough and simple, made from carved cowhide. The carving is not very delicate, and in many places, it is not carved with a knife but directly painted. This combination of carving and painting is one of the unique features of Ji'nan shadow puppetry. The height of the puppets is about one *Chi* (1 *Chi*=0.328,084 meter), and the characters are divided into different roles such as Sheng (old and young male roles), Dan (female roles), Jing (painted face roles), and Chou (comic roles). Among the characters, most of the bookmen have only one arm, while the warriors have two arms. For the horse-riding

Ji'nan Shadow Play
冀南皮影

puppets, the upper body is movable, while the lower body is carved together with the horse as a whole. Folk artists' handling of the puppet's shape, color, and carving is not only based on the generalization and exaggeration of the character's required features but also influenced by folk paper-cutting and theatrical facial makeup. At the same time, it gradually forms a stylized and role-specific modeling system. Ji'nan shadow puppetry performances have no written scripts and are entirely passed down orally. The dialogues are colloquial and easy to understand, with distinctive local characteristics.

Ji'nan shadow puppetry largely retains the early appearance of Chinese shadow puppetry. Compared to Tangshan shadow puppetry, it has very strong differences in terms of character design, scripts, singing styles, and performance forms, possessing high academic value and cultural connotations.

Hejian Shadow Puppetry

Hejian shadow puppetry is an important representative of central Hebei shadow puppetry, which is the spread of western Chinese shadow puppetry in the North China Plain. It is said to have been brought by migrants from Gansu and Shaanxi during the Ming Dynasty, and folk artists call it "Lanzhou(capital of Gansu Province) Shadow". It is mainly popular in the areas of Baoding, Cangzhou, Langfang, and Shijiazhuang of Hebei. Currently, central Hebei shadow puppetry has basically disappeared in places like Baoding and Langfang, while it is still relatively well-preserved in Hejian.

The carving of Hejian shadow puppets is exquisite, with graceful and lifelike shapes. They serve not only as props for shadow puppet performances but also as folk handicrafts with local characteristics. Hejian shadow puppet troupes maintain traditional customs. Every autumn, they perform shadow puppetry to pray for blessings, pay homage to the gods, and serve as a form of entertainment for the villagers.

◫ Chapter 22
Cangzhou Martial Arts
—The Hometown of Chinese Martial Arts

Cangzhou, known as the "Hometown of Martial Arts", has a long history of producing heroes and elites for thousands of years. According to statistics, Cangzhou produced 1,937 Wujinshi (武进士) and Wujuren (武举人) during the Ming and Qing dynasties[1]. There

Cangzhou Martial Arts
沧州武术

---

[1] "Wujinshi" and "Wujuren" are titles given to those who passed the imperial martial arts examinations in ancient China. These examinations were held to select talented individuals for military positions in the government. Wujinshi refers to those who passed the highest level of the martial arts examination, while Wujuren refers to those who passed the lower level of the examination. These titles were highly respected and represented a person's martial arts skills and achievements.

are as many as 52 types of martial arts and martial art equipment originating and spreading in Cangzhou, accounting for 40% of the 129 types of martial arts and martial art equipment in China. In 1992, as one of the birthplaces of Chinese martial arts, Cangzhou was named as the "Hometown of Martial Arts" by the National Sports Commission in the first batch, becoming the first prefecture-level city in China to win this honor.

Cangzhou martial arts have their own unique characteristics, featuring both bold and powerful moves as well as nimble and flexible techniques in pushing hands① and grappling② They are known for their fast speed, strong force, and excellent offensive and defensive capabilities in actual combat. Martial arts can be roughly divided into two major factions: Shaolin and Wudang. Shaolin boxing includes various styles such as Bajiquan, Taizu Changquan, and Liuhequan, while Wudang boxing includes Taijiquan, Baguaquan, and Xingyiquan.

In recent years, under the guidance of the national policy of "exploring, researching, organizing, and inheriting" martial arts, Cangzhou martial arts have gained new vitality. Now, martial arts associations at all levels in Cangzhou have been established, with hundreds of amateur martial arts activity centers being restored and established, and tens of thousands of people participating in martial arts activities. Many veteran martial artists actively respond to the call of the state, and while teaching their skills to apprentices, they also write some books to share their knowledge.

Founded in 1989, the Cangzhou Martial Arts Festival is the earliest martial arts festival held in China and has the most competition and performance events among all mass martial arts festivals. It enjoys a high reputation both at home and abroad. The festival integrates martial arts, culture, and economy, highlights the characteristics and advantages of traditional martial arts in Cangzhou, and fully reflects the traditional, academic, and international nature of the festival that caters to the masses.

① Pushing hands, also known as "Tui Shou" in Chinese, is a training method commonly used in internal martial arts, particularly in Tai Chi.
② Grappling, also known as "Qinna" in Chinese, is a skill in Chinese martial arts mainly used for subduing, controlling, or defeating opponents.

The festival has invited enthusiasts from Russia, the United States, Belgium, Japan, Singapore and other countries and regions to participate in the "International Conference on Traditional Martial Arts", the "International Martial Arts Friendship Seminar", martial arts competitions, performances and other events, proposing to carry forward the spirit of "patriotism, self-cultivation, justice, altruism" and carrying forward the fine tradition that "all martial arts factions constitute a big family", which has expanded the influence of Cangzhou as the "Hometown of Martial Arts".

🀫 Chapter 23
Wuqiao Acrobatics
—The Cradle of Chinese Acrobatics

Wuqiao County is located in the southeastern part of Hebei Province and has a profound acrobatic culture, making it one of the birthplaces of acrobatics in China. China is regarded as the "Kingdom of Acrobatics", and Chinese acrobatics are known as the "Pearl of Eastern Art", largely due to the acrobatics inherited by this small county and the brilliance created by its acrobatics. On May 20, 2006, Wuqiao acrobatics were approved by the State Council to be included in the first batch of the National Intangible Cultural Heritage List.

In Wuqiao County, acrobatic art is commonly known as "juggling". As the folk rhyme goes, "From the elderly at ninety-nine to the children who have just learned to walk, everyone in Wuqiao is a master of juggling." People in Wuqiao have a special fondness for acrobatics. Whether on the streets, in the fields, or even at the dinner tables and on the kangs ("kang", a

Wuqiao acrobatics
吴桥杂技

traditional Chinese heated bed), they will perform somersaults, stack Arhats[1], practice boxing, and perform various magic tricks at any time.

"No Wuqiao, no acrobatic troupe" is a widely circulated saying in the acrobatics industry. It means that an acrobatic troupe cannot be formed without acrobats from Wuqiao. This saying has two implications. First, there are many acrobats from Wuqiao, so naturally, there are people from Wuqiao in every acrobatic troupe. Second, the skills of Wuqiao artists are excellent, and it is difficult to support an acrobatic troupe without them. Wuqiao not only has a long history of acrobatics and many relevant cultural relics, but it has also produced many famous acrobats and acrobatic troupes in modern Chinese history. The emergence of these famous figures and troupes demonstrates Wuqiao's enormous contribution to Chinese acrobatics. Wuqiao is the cradle of Chinese acrobatic artists. Generations of people from Wuqiao have devoted their lives and energy to the cause of acrobatics, and with extraordinary perseverance and dedication to the acrobatic career, they have promoted the continuous development of acrobatic art throughout history.

After the implementation of the reform and opening-up policy, the state has given high attention and support to Wuqiao acrobatics. This has stimulated the enthusiasm of the people of Wuqiao to promote acrobatic culture and develop the Wuqiao economy, and acrobatics have since entered a prosperous stage of rapid development.

In November 1993, the Wuqiao Acrobatics World was completed and opened to the public. The southern part of it is an ancient-style architectural complex including the Jianghu Culture City, the Lyuzu Temple, the Sun Gong Temple, and the Taishan Palace; the northern part is surrounded by a modern architectural complex including the Acrobatics Wonder Palace, the Magic Illusion Palace, etc., embracing the magnificent central square. Connected from north to south by 16 towering marble totem poles of acrobatic history, the bird's-eye view of the entire area resembles an acrobatic unicycle, reflecting not only the development history of Wuqiao acrobatics but also its extraordinary and grand atmosphere. In 2004, Wuqiao was named as one of the first batch of "Hometown of Chinese Acrobatics" by the state.

---

[1] Stacking Arhats is a Chinese acrobatic performance in which performers support and stack on top of each other to form a highly stacked human structure.

Chapter 24
Quyang Stone Carving

—An Unparalleled Beauty Crafted Through Two Thousand Years of Hammering and Chiseling

Quyang is the hometown of Chinese stone carving art, with white stone carving being particularly famous. Starting from the Western Han Dynasty, people in Quyang began to mine local white stones and embarked on the path of carving. This is where the so-called Han Baiyu (white marble) comes from. According to research, the white marble male and female figurines unearthed from the tomb of Liu Sheng (King of Zhongshan, with the posthumous title of "Jing") in the Western Han Dynasty in Mancheng (a district of Baoding) were carved from Quyang Huangshan white marble, making them the oldest Quyang stone carving works discovered so far. The Dog Pagoda in Wangtaibei Village of Quyang is said to have been built by Liu Xiu, Emperor Guangwu of the Eastern Han Dynasty, for a loyal dog. The 13-floor Dog Pagoda is about 50

Side relief of the Monument to the People's Heroes
人民英雄纪念碑侧面浮雕

meters high, and is made of finely crafted Huangshan white marble and bricks. The stone walls of the first to fourth floors of the pagoda are engraved with relief murals, which are well-structured, evenly laid out, and highly artistic, representing the artistic level of Quyang stone carvers at that time. The Dog Pagoda of Quyang is one of the earliest monumental large-scale stone carving buildings in China and a building with a high level of stone carving art achievement during the Eastern Han Dynasty.

During the Wei, Jin, and Southern and Northern Dynasties, Buddhism flourished, and temples were built and caves were carved all over the country on a large scale, with unprecedented grandeur. As a result, Quyang stone carving developed rapidly during this period. At that time, Quyang stone carvers traveled all over the country, fully utilizing their carving talents to create numerous Buddhist statues.

During the Sui and Tang Dynasties, Quyang stone carvings tended to be mature and natural, with figures either tall and strong or graceful and charming, elegant and magnificent, creating a unique style. The plump and full-bodied female performers in the music and dance paintings unearthed from the tomb of Wang Chuzhi during the Five Dynasties, as well as the imposing and powerful door gods in relief, are impressive and not inferior to those of the prosperous Tang Dynasty, which are rarely seen in the world. During this period, Quyang stone carving entered a stage of rapid development, and Quyang thus became the carving center of northern China.

In the Yuan Dynasty, Yang Qiong, who represented the highest level of Quyang stone carving, presided over the construction of Dadu, the capital of the Yuan Dynasty. The stone carving art flourished in the field of architecture, which has opened up a new direction and influenced all generations to come.

During the Ming and Qing Dynasties, in the construction of royal palaces, tombs, and gardens, Quyang stone carvers fully demonstrated their exquisite carving skills, almost reaching the pinnacle of their craft. On the two revetment stones on the north bank of Suzhou Street in the Summer Palace, there are inscriptions of "Quyang Craftsmen", which serve as precious historical materials of Quyang stone carvers' participation in the garden construction of the capital.

In the early days of the founding of the People's Republic of China, more than a dozen Quyang carving artists were selected and sent to Beijing. After more than a year of training, they were responsible for the main carving tasks of the relief on the Monument to the People's Heroes. After the completion of the monument, following the instructions of Premier Zhou Enlai, the Beijing Municipal Government established the Beijing Architectural Art Carving Factory with the Quyang carving artists who participated in the construction of the monument as the backbone. This provided a broader stage for Quyang carving artists to display their talents.

When creating gender-ambiguous figures such as Buddha statues, Quyang stone carvings emphasize the depiction of the inner world of the characters and pays attention to the interaction and harmony between characters and between characters and animals. Quyang stone carvings focus on the charm of the figures, not just their appearance. They remove tedious details, focus on the spirit of the characters and the gist of the structure, and use subtraction to achieve a vivid representation in the dynamic structure. Quyang stone carving works have various shapes and compositions, and due to the primitive means of stone mining, it is impossible to control the thickness, thinness, and shape of the stone materials. Quyang stone carving artists adapt their creations to the shape of the materials, using their rich imagination to carve a variety of stone works based on these stones of irregular shapes.

In Quyang stone carvings, various techniques such as round carving, relief carving, and line engraving are often mixed and used flexibly in a large-scale stone carving, with some parts featuring relief and line engraving. In Quyang stone carving works, the head and hands of the figures are round carvings, while most of the body is in the form of high relief attached to the stone wall, and the details of clothing and accessories are expressed through line engraving. Inlay and openwork techniques are sometimes also incorporated.

The cultural connotation of Quyang stone carving is profound. It embodies the carving spirit of generations of ancient and simple farmers and craftsmen who mainly relied on agriculture for their livelihood in the Taihang Mountains. They extensively absorbed the nourishment of the

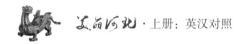

cultures of various ethnic groups in the north and Buddhism, and integrated a strong national spirit into their works. These works are imbued with the Quyang carving craftsmen's deep understanding of life, their unique insights into the art of stone carving, and their national cultural pride, religious beliefs, and aesthetic tastes, which are integrated in each statue. Throughout history, the Quyang stone carving works of various periods have demonstrated Quyang craftsmen' ingenious carving techniques that hide delicacy within simplicity, use small details to represent larger concepts, and bring life to seemingly unyielding stones. They contain the profound connotation of Quyang culture and have great inheritance value. In this area rich in white stone, Quyang people have continuously carved with their hammers and chisels, and have created numerous world-class cultural treasures, making Quyang stone carving thrive for more than two thousand years with its unique charm and vitality.

🎋 Chapter 25
Jingxing Lahua

—A Graceful and Well-proportioned Folk Dance Art

Jingxing Lahua is a unique folk art form widely spread in the villages of Jingxing County, Shijiazhuang City. Since ancient times, it has been deeply loved by the local people for its profound and simple charm, strong and desolate artistic features, and expressive dance postures. It can be said that "From the age of ninety-nine to those who have just learned to walk, everyone can perform it." On May 20, 2006, Jingxing Lahua was approved by the State Council to be included in the first batch of the National Intangible Cultural Heritage List.

Jingxing Lahua
井陉拉花

Jingxing Lahua originated from street "flower gatherings"[1] during festivals, temple fairs, and foundation-laying and deity-worshipping ceremonies. It has a long history and a far-reaching influence. There is no historical record or written evidence to determine when and where Lahua was created and formed. By the early 20th century, Lahua had become very popular and had become a well-received dance form among the local people, with the saying that "As frequently as you can hear Shanxi Bangzi (a local opera of Shanxi Province) sung by people all the time, you can see Jingxing Lahua dancers dancing everywhere." In 1996, the Ministry of Culture of the People's Republic of China named Jingxing County as the "Hometown of Chinese Folk Art—Hometown of Lahua".

This dance was formed in a natural environment characterized by "seeing mountains as soon as you step out of the door and climbing slopes when walking". Therefore, its dance postures show the characteristics of walking on the high mountains and steep roads in Jingxing, reflecting the scenes of walking on bumpy and winding mountain roads, lifting legs high, moving forward and backward, bending forward and backward, swaying left and right, going up and down, navigating twists and turns, supporting each other, and facing difficulties head-on.

Its music is also an independent genre. It has the charm of Hebei blow-songs[2], the tunes of folk songs, folk tunes, and opera tunes, as well as the rich colors of temple music and court music. There are about a dozen tunes, such as "Eternal Happiness" "The Four Seasons", and "Ivy". It is simple and elegant, refreshing and pleasant, profound and beautiful, robust and steady. Its stylistic features are firm but not wild, soft but not weak, gorgeous but not frivolous, sad but not tearful, with a distinct rhythm. The music complements the steady, restrained, robust, and bold style of Lahua dance, blending music and dance into a harmonious whole.

Jingxing Lahua has remarkable artistic features. It takes "twist shoulder" "twist wrist" "twist arm" "suck leg" and "skim foot" as the main

---

[1] "flower gathering" is a general term for various recreational activities held during festivals. It is an ancient folk tradition.

[2] "Hebei blow-songs" are a traditional wind and percussion music popular in Hebei Province. They mainly feature wind instruments, supplemented by percussion instruments and string instruments. Most of the performed pieces are derived from traditional folk songs and opera singing.

dance movements, with "vase" "flower umbrella" "color fan" and "overlord whip" as the main performance props.

Jingxing Lahua has distinctive artistic features, with "twisting shoulders" "flipping wrists" "twisting arms" "sucking legs", and "flicking feet" as the main dance movements. The main performance props include "flower vases" "flower umbrellas" "colorful fans", and "Bawangbian (a rattle stick used in folk dancing)". Accompanied by Lahua music, which can be considered an independent genre, it forms a unique artistic style that combines both softness and strength, and is both rough and subtle. It is adept at expressing emotions such as sadness, desolation, nostalgia, and joy.

Jingxing Lahua is a group dance that is not restricted by the venue. It can be performed on the streets, in courtyards, or on stages, with varying durations. There are two types of performances: one is a performance during a procession, called "crossing the street". This type of performance is limited by the procession and cannot achieve the completeness of the dance, but it has the characteristic of adapting to the environment. The other type is a venue performance, with various formations that fully showcase the performers' skills and present a complete performance. The number of performers participating in the performance is generally a multiple of six, and large-scale Lahua teams such as 18-person Lahua, 36-person Lahua, 60-person Lahua, and 102-person Lahua all inherit this characteristic.

🀄 Chapter 26
Hebei Bangzi

—A Melody Lingering in the Land of Yan-Zhao

Hebei Bangzi is the main local opera in Hebei Province and an important branch of Chinese Bangzi vocal style, formed during the reign of Emperor Daoguang of the Qing Dynasty. It was developed by the people of Hebei after the "Shanxi-Shaanxi Bangzi" was introduced to the region. Hebei Bangzi is popular in Hebei, Tianjin, Beijing, as well as parts of Shandong, Henan, and Shanxi, making it one of the most influential traditional opera genres in northern China. On May 20, 2006, Hebei Bangzi was approved by the State Council to be included in the first batch of the National Intangible Cultural Heritage List.

Baolian Lamp
河北梆子《宝莲灯》剧照

Hebei Bangzi is not only good at expressing historical themes but also adept at reflecting real life. Currently, there are more than 500 traditional plays preserved, some of which expose the decay and ugliness of the feudal ruling class, some reflect class oppression, some praise the heroic figures in the anti-invasion wars, some admire women's pursuit and longing for marriage freedom, and some depict the humor in rural life.

Its traditional plays are mostly based on historical stories, with representative works including *The Butterfly Cup, Qin Xianglian, Killing the Son at the Gate, and Du Shiniang*.

In 2018, the Beijing Hebei Bangzi Opera Troupe created and launched an original large-scale modern Hebei Bangzi play, *The Monument to the People's Heroes,* as a tribute to the 70th anniversary of the founding of the People's Republic of China. The play is a work that "sings the praises of the Party, the motherland, the people, and the heroes". It is the first concrete and artistic interpretation of the Monument to the People's Heroes, the spiritual symbol of the Chinese nation, embodying the creative sentiment of artists in the new era who are committed to remembering their origins, remaining true to the original aspiration, paying tribute to the people and heroes, and providing a resting place for the souls of the people's heroes.

The Monument to the People's Heroes tells the story of Yuqin, a military representative who returns to her hometown Dashi Village in Quyang county, Hebei Province in the spring of 1952 to recruit stone carvers to carve the Monument to the People's Heroes. With Yuqin's efforts, the indispensable master stone carver, Shi Laodie, puts aside all personal grudges and devotes himself to the carving of the monument.

Exercises

Ⅰ. Comprehension

（1）What are the differences between the paper-cutting of Yuxian County and other paper-cutting styles? What other regional paper-cutting arts are you familiar with?

（2）Chinese acrobatics are divided into two schools, the northern school is Wuqiao acrobatics, but what is the southern school of acrobatics?

（3）In addition to the shadow puppetry introduced in this part, please find out more shadow puppetry from other regions.

（4）Please research and find out, in which provinces are China's famous stone carving schools distributed?

Ⅱ. Translation

1. Term Translation

（1）文房四宝

（2）武能上马安天下，文能提笔定乾坤

（3）蔚县打树花

（4）内画鼻烟壶

2. Passage Translation

石头，没有生命，但落到匠人的手中，却偏偏被赋予了灵魂与文化的生气。一锤、一打，剥落、打磨，石头便有了灵魂。我们能看到的有关曲阳石雕工艺年代最久远的作品，是满城汉墓出土的 5 件汉白玉男女俑。在此后千年的发展中，曲阳石雕出现在了许多我们熟悉的地方，赵州桥、曲阳北岳庙等地，都有曲阳石雕的身影，就连人民英雄纪念碑上，都有曲阳石雕的工艺。

中文部分

第1篇
魅力河北　燕赵大地

　　"于山则太行之峻，于水则浑河之险，于野则广川大陵之雄，于隍堡则卢龙雕鹗之隘，于关塞则居庸扼其前，独石阻其背。于陆泽之所产，则黍菽之殖，鱼盐之利。于土风则犹有击筑卖浆慷慨悲歌之习……"这是清朝康熙年间《畿辅通志》中对河北省的描述。河北，因地处黄河下游以北而得名的省份，在全国范围内和其他省份相比较，其地理位置的独特之处就在于其内环京津，这一方面削弱了河北省内空间联系的整体性，另一方面又铸就了京津冀三者关系的紧密性。河北，地处我国东部地带，在交通运输上具有"东出西联"的便利，是首都与全国各地陆路交通的必经之地；在文化上呈现出燕赵和京畿两个文化亚区相互重叠的特色，既有古人的慷慨悲歌，又有现代人的无私奉献。

第1章

河北的地理特征

——倚太行临渤海，屏燕山俯沃野

河北省位于东经 113° 27′ 至 119° 50′，北纬 36° 03′ 至 42° 37′ 之间；南北长 730 千米，东西宽 560 千米；地处华北腹地，东临渤海，西倚太行，北为燕山山地，燕山以北兼跨内蒙古高原，中部为河北平原，面积 18.88 万平方千米；环绕北京和天津两座直辖市，东南部、南部衔接山东、河南两省，西部隔太行山与山西省为邻，西北部与内蒙古自治区交界，东北部与辽宁省接壤。下辖石家庄、唐山、邯郸、保定、沧州、廊坊、衡水、邢台、张家口、承德、秦皇岛 11 个地级市，省会石家庄。

河北省所处的大地构造属于内蒙古地槽南缘，中朝准地台北部。反映在地貌上，北部为坝上高原，属于内蒙古高原的南缘，燕山和太行山两大山脉形成半环状，环抱河北平原；燕山以南、太行山以东为河北平原。鸟瞰河北大地，其地形走势与整个中国地形特征一致，西北高，东南低，三级阶梯界限显著。河北境内最大海拔落差超过 2 500 米，既有巍巍的高山，又有山间盆地；既有起伏不平的高原、丘陵，又有广阔的平原，其间有许多洼淀，又有湿地分布，地貌类型齐全，类型特征鲜明。

河北西北部的坝上高原面积为 1.6 万平方千米，占全省地表总面积的 8.5%。坝上高原与内蒙古高原相连，平均海拔为 1 200 ～ 1 500 米，地势高耸，起伏不大，呈现"远看是山，近看是川"的景象。高原上多湖、淖、滩、梁，有广阔的天然草地。

河北省的山地主要由燕山和太行山两大山脉组成，如果把丘陵和山间盆地面积计算在内，总面积约有 9.01 万平方千米，占全省地表总面积的 48.1%。燕山山脉横亘于北部，呈东西走向，岩性复杂多样，山地因岩性不同而形态各异，形成千姿百态的奇峰异石。燕山是滦河和潮白河等多条河流的发源地。太行山脉位于河北省西部，其主体部分呈东北—西南走向，是河北省与山西省的天然界限。由于太行山脉地质条件复杂，使这里的地表形态千差万别。主体山脉海拔为 1 000 ～ 1 500 米，小五台山位于太行山北端，海拔2 882 米，为河北省第一高峰。

太行山以东和燕山以南的平原区是华北平原的一部分，总面积约 8.16 万平方千米，占全省地表总面积的 43.4%。平原地区地势不高，海拔多在百米以下，低于 50 米的占绝大部分。在河北平原上，分布着许多洼地，总面积达 1 000 平方千米。在保定与天津大沽之间，是河北平原北部低洼地分布中心，著名的白洋淀、文安洼和大洼就分布在这一带。

河北省河流众多，长度在 18 千米以上 1 000 千米以下者就达 300 多条。境内河流大都发源或流经燕山、冀北山地和太行山山区，其下游有的合流入海，有的单独入海，还有因地形流入湖泊不外流者。主要河流从南到北依次有漳卫南运河、子牙河、大清河、永定河、潮白河、蓟运河、滦河、阴河、乌拉岱河、老哈河等，分属海河、滦河、内陆河、辽河、滨海小水系等五大水系。

在全国近 2 万千米大陆海岸线中，河北 487 千米海岸线长度并不突出，但在河北所管辖的海岸线上，有秦皇岛、唐山、沧州等密集的港口群及沿海产业园区，从北向南依次为秦皇岛港、唐山港（含京唐港和曹妃甸港）、黄骅港。这三个港口各有特点：秦皇岛港作为全国北煤南运枢纽港，转型发展集装箱运输和邮轮母港；唐山港是面向东北亚开放的桥头堡，打造服务重大国家战略的能源原材料主枢纽港；黄骅港辐射冀中六市，是雄安新区最便捷的出海口。

大自然独特的自然禀赋，让河北省成为中国唯一兼有高原、山地、丘陵、沙漠、盆地、平原、河流、湖泊和海滨的省份。因此，有人形容河北地势为山脉如镰，河流如扇，平原如毯，海洋如盘，堪称中国地貌类型的"博物馆"，浓缩的"国家地理读本"。

邯郸涉县王金庄村与旱作梯田

![第2章图标] **第 2 章**

河北的历史沿革

——从古冀州到京畿重地的变迁

冀州，是汉籍《尚书·禹贡》所描述的汉地九州之一，书中记载大禹分天下为九州，冀州位列九州之首，包括现在的北京市、天津市、河北省、山西省、河南省北部及辽宁省与内蒙古自治区部分地区。

"河北"的名称则出自唐代"河北道"。河北大地的代称"燕赵"则来自更早的先秦。

百家争鸣的春秋战国时期，奠定了中国区域文化格局：燕赵之于河北（京津冀）、齐鲁之于山东、吴越之于江浙、三晋之于山西、三秦之于陕西、巴蜀之于川渝的对应，都是源于当时的古国名称。

春秋时期，河北是燕赵争雄之地：北方最强的诸侯国晋国被韩赵魏三家瓜分继承，赵国原本的都城在高原盆地中的晋阳（今山西省太原市），后将都城迁到河北平原上的邯郸。赵国鼎盛时期，其疆域远大于今日河北省的行政区划，腹地为河北中部、南部；今河北北部及北京、天津地区为燕国所有。燕赵大地，其实是包括京津在内的大河北地区。

公元前 221 年，秦朝统一中国后，实行郡县制，在河北境内陆续设置了上谷、渔阳、右北平、广阳、邯郸、巨鹿、代、恒山八郡。

汉至隋，河北大地分属幽、冀二州：幽州西南与冀州覆盖今河北地区。

唐代设立河北道，构成今河北省的基本版图，也是现在河北省省名的源头。

宋、金时期，河北路继承河北道，后又拆分为河北西路、河北东路。

元、明、清三朝，河北是京畿腹地，华夏首省。元代实行行省制度，位于元朝大都（今北京）附近的今河北大部为"腹里"地区，归中央中书省直辖。明代在元代行省制度基础上设置北直隶省，奠定了今日河北版图的轮廓。清代则将原北直隶省改为直隶省，版图略有变化。

近现代，河北版图变化频繁，但大的格局未变，最终成了今天的模样。

从战国时期燕赵腹地到今天的河北区域，虽然面积常有变化，但核心部分比较稳定，那就是太行山与燕山东南那片广袤的平原。华北平原在河北的部分，一般称为河北平原，因主要在海河流域，也称海河平原。

华北平原是中华文明重要的发祥地和繁衍地之一。宋代之前的经济文化重心地区，河北是其中不可或缺的组成部分。

北以燕山为屏、西以太行为靠，两道大山与平原棱线，组成了一个巨大的倒"L"或倒"J"——这也是河北省的主体轮廓。

河北平原是中原的组成部分，河北北部山区则是农牧文明交错交融的地带，燕山与太行山两道屏障，是历代王朝倚重的天然长城。它的南部是中原重要腹地的组成部分，与河南、山东连成广袤肥沃的华北平原，一直是北方地区历史文化最灿烂、经济最发达的区域。

京津冀共同的母亲河——海河是一个庞大的水系：它由五大支流组成，即潮白河、永定河、大清河、子牙河、南运河，这五条河在天津市区三岔河口汇入海河。整个海河水系所覆盖的区域，就像一把大扇子。

在天津登上历史舞台之前的三四千年里，海河中上游早已创造了诸多辉煌。海河流域孕育的安阳、邯郸、大同、张家口，以及石家庄周边的灵寿、正定、定州等都是拥有两三千年历史的古城。

河北境内的城市座落于太行山东麓一线，这里就是海河冲积扇连起来的文明走廊、城市带，就是这一线，"南北大道"也由它们连缀而成。

无论是从长安、洛阳、开封等北方都城向南开拓，还是从杭州、南京等南方都城向北交流，都必须走这条山前大道。今天京广铁路就是这条大道的现代版，中国南北主要的重镇，几乎都在这条大道上。

至少从春秋战国开始，燕地重镇蓟（今北京）与中原古都殷（今安阳）之间，就形成了一条南北畅通的大道。秦灭六国后实行"车同轨"，开辟的驰道中，其中一条就连接着今北京与安阳地区。从古道基础上发展而来的公路，现在是京港澳高速的北段，由京石、石安组成；平汉、京广铁路，也穿过这条古老的交通要道。

这条大道上，分布着河北、北京地区的都城：商代邢都（今邢台），春秋战国燕下都（今易县）、中山都（今灵寿、定州）、赵国都城（今邯郸），曹魏后期至北朝的都城邺城（今临漳县西），辽、宋、金、元、明、清古都北京。其中，邯郸南部的邺城经历两朝建都，堪称"小六朝古都"。随着北齐灭亡，旧邺城化为废墟，邺城的文化转向漳河南岸的安阳——安阳，正是这条大道的南部终点。

战国时期至汉代的河北，"战国七雄"的燕、赵双雄的都城都在河北区域，还有一个"二线"诸侯国中山国；司马迁在《史记·货殖列传》中提到了战国到西汉时期全国有 9 个经济"都会"，京津冀地区有蓟、邯郸，放到今天就是国家中心城市级别。

魏晋北朝的河北，境内的邺城充当过战乱中六个王朝的都城。当长安洛阳在战乱中变成一片狼藉时，河北南部的邺城是乱世中短暂安宁的北方经济中心。邺城地区的古城及相关文物出土，证明了那曾经是一座经济繁华、文化并包的大都会。

曹操诗中的"铜雀台"，就是邺城著名的标志建筑。

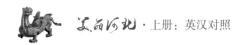

隋唐时期河北没有王朝都城，但依旧是王朝的经济发达地区，并拥有充当了当时"国家走廊"的交通动脉，在既有传统太行山前陆路大道基础上，开辟了一条运河大道。这就是一条从幽州（今北京）到贝州（今清河县）的大运河。

此后河北地区地位发生变化，但依然重要，只是舞台上的主角换成了脱胎于河北地区的北京。很多人谈论河北，总是将北京剥离开来，这是曲解。无论地理还是文化，北京跟河北都是一个整体。

中古之前的河北平原尚未出现今天的生态环境问题，经济潜力尚大，所以在为长安洛阳输血的同时，自己本身也很富裕。除了经济，那时河北所出人才也是多如繁星。北宋的陪都——北京大名府（位于今邯郸大名县）是河北地区都城最后的辉煌，随后，北京（本身也属燕赵文化区域范畴）迎来了君临天下的荣耀：辽南京—金中都—元大都—明清北京城。

宋代之前，河北平原是重要的经济文化中心，风云人物人才辈出，经济文化两开花；宋代之后，河北地区主要充当政治和军事重地，成为北京最重要的前沿，曾经辉煌无比的太行山东麓的南北大道，在经济上只能充当了运输走廊的功能。延续到近代，它的省域版图不知道调整了多少次，直隶与河北名称来回改变，省会在天津、保定、石家庄之间变动。

一路走来，从绚烂到平静再到沉默——燕赵大地慷慨悲歌的传统，一直贯穿在河北大地和河北人民身上。沉淀数千年的慷慨悲歌与浩然之气，依然在每个燕赵儿女的心头燃烧。

第3章
河北的气候特征
——四季分明，物产丰富

　　河北省地处中纬度欧亚大陆东岸，属于温带半湿润半干旱大陆性季风气候。大部分地区四季分明，寒暑悬殊，干湿季明显。具有冬季寒冷干旱，雨雪稀少，春季冷暖多变，干旱多风；夏季烈日炎炎，雨量集中；秋季风和日丽，凉爽少雨的特点。省内总体气候条件较好，温度适宜，日照充沛，热量丰富，雨热同期，适合多种农作物和林果的生长。

　　河北省年平均气温由北向南逐渐升高，冀北高原年平均气温低于4℃，以御道口最低，为-0.3℃。中南部地区年平均气温上升至12℃以上，以峰峰矿区最高，达14℃。南北年平均气温相差甚为悬殊。全省年极端最高气温多出现在6月，长城以南最高可以达

黄骅勃海开渔

到 40℃ 以上。南部平原气温超过 35℃ 的酷热日达 18 ～ 25 天。中部平原及南太行山区为 10 ～ 18 天。唐山秦皇岛地区沿海及北部山区只有 1 ～ 4 天。冀北高原没有酷热天气。年极端最低气温主要在冀北高原，达 −30℃ 以下。

河北省湿地资源丰富，类型众多，既有浅海、滩涂，又有陆地河流、水库、湖泊及洼地，具有重要的资源、气候和科研价值。全省湿地面积占全省土地总面积的 59%，比全国的平均水平 27% 高一倍多。湿地相对集中分布在沿海、坝上地区，平原地区、广大山区只有零星分布。其中被列入国家林业局"中国重要湿地名录"的有昌黎黄金海岸湿地、滦河口湿地、白洋淀湿地、北戴河沿海湿地、沧州南大港湿地、张家口坝上湿地（张北县安固里淖）和衡水湖湿地。由于湿地类型众多，植物群落类型多样，为不同生态类型的野生动物提供了适宜的栖息环境，同时这些湿地也成为众多迁徙鸟类途中停息和补充能量的栖息地。

河北省成矿地质条件优越，矿产资源比较丰富。现已发现各类矿产 159 种，已探明储量的矿产 133 种，其中保有储量居全国大陆省份前六位的达 39 种。大宗矿产如煤、铁、石油（天然气）、金、各种石灰岩等为河北省优势矿产。河北省煤炭产量居全国第三位，煤炭品种较齐全，以炼焦用煤为主，集中分布在唐山、邯郸、邢台、张家口等地；铁矿主要分布于太行山和燕山山区，探明储量居全国第三位，并且与冶金辅助原料组合良好；河北省也是中国六大金矿集中分布区之一，金矿产量居全国第三位，主产地位于承德；石油、天然气资源主要分布在河北平原的中部和东部以及冀东沿海地区；石灰岩矿产资源丰富，种类多，质量好。

在新能源方面，地热资源大都集中于中北部地区，这一区域总计可采资源量折合标煤 110.5 亿吨，仅次于西藏、云南，居全国第三位，中低温地下热水资源居全国之首。全省有开发价值的热水点 241 处，其中山区 92 处，平均水温 40 ～ 70℃，其余分布于平原，水温最高可达 95 ～ 118℃。风能资源地区分布差异悬殊，且季节变化明显。除坝上及沿海狭小地区风能资源丰富外，广大山区及河北平原大部风能资源欠缺。河北太阳能资源仅次于青藏及西北地区，年辐射量为 4 981 ～ 5 966 兆焦 / 平方米，年日照时数张家口、承德及沧州东部为 2 800 ～ 3 000 小时，为全省最多的地区，邢台、邯郸西部及中部为 2 500 ～ 2 600 小时，是全省最少的地区；其他大部分地区为 2 600 ～ 2 750 小时，日照率为 50% ～ 70%。

河北省的动物资源比较丰富。有陆栖（包括两栖）脊椎动物 530 余种，约占全国同类动物种类的 29.0%，其中兽类接近 80 种，约占全国兽类种数的 21.5%；鸟类 420 余种，约占全国鸟类种数的 36.1%，有不少全国珍贵、稀有种类，如鸟类中的褐马鸡、白冠长尾鸡、天鹅等，其中褐马鸡为我国特有的珍稀动物，国内仅见于河北省与山西省。爬行类、两栖类分别有 19 种和 10 种，其中属于国家一类保护的动物有兽类 1 种（华北豹）。省内现有家畜家禽 100 多个品种，其中张北马、阳原驴、草原红牛、武安羊、冀南牛、深州猪等均为驰名省内外的优良品种。河北沿海所产鱼类有 110 多种，较主要的有带鱼、黄花鱼、梭鱼、比目鱼、鲆鱼、鲳鱼以及著名的香鱼等。秦皇岛一带所产的头索动物文昌鱼属国家二类保护动物。海产虾类 20 多种，以对虾最为有名，琵琶虾的产量最大，蟹类 10 多种，贝类中较主要的有文蛤、青蛤、蛏、蚶及牡蛎等，棘皮动物海参也有一定产量。省内淡水面积约 120 万亩。经济价值较大的淡水鱼有草鱼、鲢鱼、鳙鱼、鲤鱼、鲫鱼、鲂鱼、黑鱼、鳝鱼、鳜鱼及细鳞鱼等。还有不少淡水虾、蟹出产。

河北省地处暖温带与温带的交界区，植被种类多样，是全国植物资源比较丰富的省区之一，据初步统计有 156 科、3 000 多种。栽培作物主要有：粮食作物小麦、玉米、谷子、水稻、高粱、豆类等，经济作物棉花、油料、麻类等。木本植物 500 多种，包括用材树 100 多种，驰名中外的树种有二青杨、香椿、栓皮栎等，经济价值较高的树种有云杉、油松、柏树、华北落叶松、榆树、椴树、槐树、青檀、白楸及桦树等，特种经济树种漆树、杜仲、泡桐、黄连木等也有分布。全省的果树有百余种，干果主要有板栗、核桃、花椒等，板栗产量占全国总产量的 1/4，居全国第一。鲜果主要有梨、苹果、红果（山楂的别名）、杏、桃、葡萄、柿子、李子及石榴等，其中梨的产量居全国第一。

河北省果品中有很多驰名中外，如赵县雪花梨，深州蜜桃，宣化葡萄，昌黎苹果，

褐马鸡

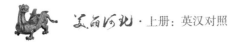

沧州金丝小枣，阜平、赞皇大枣，迁西板栗等畅销国内外。灌木的种类很多，分布较广，有些野果及药材也属灌木。草本植物的种类也很多，仅坝上地区即有300多种，包括不少优良牧草，如禾本科的羊草、无芒雀麦、冰草，豆科的紫花苜蓿、山野豌豆等。药用植物已被利用的有800多种，较主要的有葛藤、甘草、麻黄、大黄、党参、枸杞、枣仁、柴胡、防风、知母、白芷、远志、桔梗、薄荷及黄芩等。

第4章
河北的交通网络
——东出西联，京津冀交通一体化

    河北省地处我国东部地带，地处太平洋沿岸，地形上处于中国的第三级阶梯，良港众多，形成了独特的区位优势——东出西联，形成沿海和腹地、省内和省外的互动格局，能够更好地利用国际和国内两种市场及资源。

    东出，是利用河北省的港口群和沿海经济物流体系，为华北、西北各省提供便捷的出海大通道；西联，则是河北省加强了与北京、天津、山西、陕西、内蒙古等地的经贸合作，与外长城经济圈对接，实现优势互补。内环京津、外环渤海是河北独特的区位优

河北省开启中欧班列公铁海联运模式

势，东出能够让河北省充分利用 487 千米的海岸线，像上海那样发展临港工业区，建设沿海经济隆起带，融入环渤海经济区；西联则可建立与包括呼和浩特、大同、榆林、兰州、西宁等十几个城市的外长城经济圈的对接，延伸产业腹地，为环渤海经济区的制造业提供源源不断的初级产品和能源供应。

河北省是首都北京连接全国各地的交通枢纽，由北京通往全国各地的干线铁路和公路，均须经过河北向外辐射，也是沟通和联系西北、华北、东北、华南、华东等大经济区的物资交流和进出口必经之地，交通战略地位重要。

2015 年，中共中央政治局审议通过《京津冀协同发展规划纲要》。纲要指出，推动京津冀协同发展是一个重大国家战略，核心是有序疏解北京非首都功能，要在京津冀交通一体化、生态环境保护、产业升级转移等重点领域率先取得突破。

京津冀地区把交通一体化作为推进协同发展的先行领域，加快构建快速、便捷、高效、安全、大容量、低成本的互联互通综合交通网络。截至 2021 年底，河北省铁路里程达到 8 050 千米，居全国第 2 位；公路里程达到 20.95 万千米，其中高速公路总里程达到 8 087 千米，居全国第 4 位；港口年设计通过能力达到 11.3 亿吨，居全国第 3 位；通用机场新增 2 个，机场总数达到 16 个。京津冀"四纵四横一环"综合运输大通道基本形成，交通网络化格局持续优化。

京张高铁开通

雄安新区对外骨干路网全面打通。2021 年，交通运输系统全力推动雄安新区对外骨干路网建设，京雄高速、荣乌高速新线、京德一期高速公路和容易线、安大线建成投用，打通千秋之城"四纵三横"交通大动脉。

"轨道上的京津冀"打造区域交通新格局。京津城际延长线、京张高铁、京雄城际铁路、京哈高铁京承段等建成通车，城市副中心站枢纽、丰台、朝阳火车站及配套交通枢纽加紧建设，加快打造成京津冀区域一体化交通新格局，相邻城市间基本实现铁路 1.5 小时通达，京雄津保"1 小时交通圈"已经形成。

河北省与京津连通铁路达到 23 条，"轨道上的京津冀"主骨架基本成型。随着京张高铁、津秦高铁、京哈高铁、京雄城际、津保城际等建成通车，河北实现了市市通高铁。公路方面，河北与京津打通拓宽"对接路"34 条段、2 089 千米，与京津连通干线公路达到 47 条、74 个接口。首都地区环线高速、太行山高速等重点项目建成通车，河北全省高速公路通车里程达到 8 087 千米，实现县县通高速。

河北沿海的唐山港、秦皇岛港、黄骅港等大型港口，是包括北京在内的华北、西北地区的重要出海通道。河北全省沿海港口生产性泊位达 242 个，港口设计通过能力达 11.3 亿吨，年吞吐量突破 12 亿吨。河北港口已与世界 400 多个港口建立了贸易往来。天然深水良港——唐山港曹妃甸港区，拥有渤海水域中唯一不需要开挖的港池和天然航道，是中国多种泊位并存、单体工程量最大的港口，能停靠 30 万吨级的船只。秦皇岛港散货吞吐量名列世界散货港口首位。黄骅港作为冀中南地区最便捷、最经济的出海口，其多功能综合港区建设正在加速进行。机场方面，京津冀机场群布局加速完善，河北全省机场总数达到 16 个，一枢多支多点机场布局体系初步形成。

安全、便捷、高效、绿色、经济的综合交通体系基本建立，区域交通一体化的发展加快了区域各类生产要素的流通和周转速度，对京津冀区域经济发展及产业结构优化效果明显。

河北的文化特征

——相互重叠的燕赵文化与京畿文化

　　心理学家荣格提出过"集体无意识"的概念：一个种族或群体在不同的文化环境中，积累起无意识的深层结构，千百年沉淀下来，无形中提供了思维、行为的预先模式。我们要了解一个河北人的文化特征，就要穿越历史的时空，去聆听遥远的回响：燕赵大地的"集体无意识"，到底是怎样形成的。

　　河北作为华夏文明的重要发源地之一，先秦时期，在这块土地上诞生了燕文化、赵文化和中山文化。金、元建都以来，河北形成了独特的京畿文化，从远古走来的燕赵文化和京畿文化相互重叠，积淀了深厚的文化遗产，形成了现代河北独特的文化特色。

　　河北的古称是"燕赵"。这不仅是一个地理名词的沿用，春秋战国实际上塑造了我们的文化与人格，影响至今，形成了集体无意识。燕赵文化，指的是以河北地域为依托，源于历史上人与自然及人与人之间的相互关系而形成的特定生活结构体系，即河北地区形成的物质文化、制度文化，思想观念和生活方式的总称。燕赵文化作为河北最具特色的文化体系，包含了以下几方面：

　　第一，勇武任侠，慷慨悲歌，变革进取，自强不息。

　　河北的地理范围，大致以燕山、太行山、黄河、渤海四面为界。史书记载，这片地域在历史上面临的情境是"地边胡，数被寇"，是抵在农牧分界线的最前沿，时常要面临农耕与游牧两种文明的冲突和战争。这种冲突和战争，贯穿着河北的整个历史进程。最早可以追溯到炎黄二帝的阪泉之战，一直延续到了满族入主中原。作为政治的象征，康熙帝在承德建了避暑山庄和木兰围场，文明的冲突才以君临天下的融合姿态展示给世人。

　　春秋战国时期，现在的河北地域主要有燕、赵两国。此外，还有一个神秘的中山国，据说是狄人建立的王国，两次被灭，又两次复国，最终被赵武灵王主政时期的赵国所灭，归入赵国领土。燕国和赵国两国的分野和差异比较明显。燕国的历史比赵国早得多，当赵国从三家分晋中立国之时，燕国已经至少存在了 600 年。但燕国在整个西周和春秋几乎默默无闻，始终处于一种逼仄、局促、卑弱的境地，由此形成后人所说的"苦寒文化"。

战国中山国错银铜双翼神兽

等到燕国开始逆袭，时间已进入战国中后期。燕昭王在位时，经过 28 年的韬光养晦，燕国国力大增，任命乐毅为上将军，借助五国之兵，大败齐国，燕国由此让天下震动，刮目相看。但燕昭王死后，燕国迅速走下坡路。当秦赵长平之战结束以后，秦军兵临易水，燕国危在旦夕。燕太子丹想到的救国之策，是刺杀秦王。由此，他物色到了荆轲。"风萧萧兮易水寒，壮士一去兮不复还"，既是燕国的一曲挽歌，也是燕人的精神底色。

　　赵国源于三家分晋，国家重心从晋阳（今山西太原）迁移到邯郸（今河北邯郸），从以山西为主体到以河北为主体，经过了一个相对较长的时段。赵国位于四战之地，周边都是强邻，既面临诸侯国之间的兼并战争，还面临游牧民族的冲击。神奇的中山国，甚至嵌入赵国的腹心。赵武灵王在位时，为了解除国家的威胁，进行了轰轰烈烈的胡服骑射改革。在夷夏之防观念十分浓重的时代，能够主动向游牧民族学习，魄力可想而知。这次改革不仅改变了赵国的命运，也开启了汉民族与游牧民族在燕赵大地上对抗同时的另一扇窗户——民族融合。经过改革，赵武灵王灭掉了中山国，消除了心腹之患。赵国在崛起狂飙的进程中，始终以开放、包容、进取和尚武为国民精神，由此构建起赵人好气任侠的文化性格。燕赵的文化性格差异，经过秦始皇的疆域大一统和汉武帝的思想大一统两个时期，逐渐形成一个整体，在历史上被统一标识为慷慨悲歌的历史情结，成为燕赵文化的一个显著标志，"慷慨悲歌"也成为独属于河北人的精神底色。

第二，追求和合，顾全大局，豪侠与圣贤于一身。

燕赵大地的神奇之处还在于，她养育出来的侠客与好汉，并不是简单的武人，像我们所理解的四肢发达、头脑简单那种。她的土壤可以培育出儒与侠、文与武高度契合的君子。这两种品性恰恰是燕赵地域有别于其他地方的基因。战国末期赵国人荀子在儒家思想形成过程中，属于一个特立独行的人物：在孔子已经构建了"知天命"的重要性之后，荀子却破天荒地主张人定胜天；在孟子的性善论流行之时，荀子却主张性恶论……荀子的思想不同于当时儒家的道德理想主义，他重构了一个社会批判的观念体系，因而被后世称为"儒家中的游侠"。荀子是燕赵任侠文化熏陶出来的大儒，而他的思想也反哺了此后两千多年的燕赵大地。后世的邵雍、孙奇逢、颜元等燕赵儒林人物，大多在精神气质上继承了荀子侠客式的勇气和独立，"上不依附君主，中不苟同士林，下不媚俗民众，沉静而勇敢地阐述、践行着自己独特的思想和行为准则"。荀子以后，儒学的传承在燕赵几乎未曾中断。即便是在魏晋南北朝时期，当时的玄学、佛学大兴，儒学最为式微，但在燕赵大地上，儒学却依然兴盛。史书记载说，燕赵一带"士务经学，不崇佛老"。长期生活在燕赵的颜之推在《颜氏家训》中告诫子孙，千万不能放弃读圣贤书。虽然南北朝乱世，北方由异族统治，但燕赵的学统一直通过世家豪族进行传承，并进而影响了外来统治者，使其被逐步同化。从汉武帝开始，历朝历代基本都扼杀了侠客的生存空间。但在燕赵大地上，豪侠作为一种精神逐渐与士人阶层合流，从而形成独特的圣贤—豪侠人格。往上追溯，燕赵士人的这种人格气质，可以追溯到战国时的赵国名相蔺相如。在完璧归赵、渑池会盟等经典历史事件中，面对强邻秦国，这名赵国相国不按常理出牌，而是以死相逼——不是要与玉璧共碎，就是要在五步之内血溅秦王。但是，当赵国大将廉颇羞辱他的时候，蔺相如为了国家利益，又能忍辱负重。大丈夫能屈能伸，莫过于此。这种先国家后个人，虽有不同而自觉协调的精神，不但在燕赵大地，甚至在中华大地，也产生了巨大的感染力，激励了一代又一代的中国人。

第三，勤劳淳朴，虔诚礼让。

燕赵文化性格在漫长的历史中逐步积淀成型，但并非一成不变。特别是在金、元以后，燕赵境内的北京一跃而成为大一统王朝的都城，由此开启了帝都文化对燕赵文化的反向渗透。河北受到帝都文化的影响，在与本土燕赵文化的相互交融中，又有了新的发展，承德避暑山庄、遵化和易县的清代东西陵，都是京畿文化的产物。北京之外的古燕赵文化圈，基本上是元明清三代京畿重地的核心区域。到了清代，这里成为直隶省，地位独一无二。然而，直隶的重要性不代表资源的倾斜和照顾，而是意味着付出、牺牲与悲情。当帝国的都城位于长安—洛阳—开封一线时，燕赵大地直接抵在农耕与游牧的交界前沿，成为战略要地，人民的生活难以得到保障，负担和压力也比其他地方大。而当帝国的都城位于北京时，这里成了天子脚下之地，又必须承担起为帝都服务的职能，疏解帝都自然灾害，承受政治博弈影响。这里的人们在王朝秩序的规划下，渐渐收敛起任侠尚义之气，民风一点点平淡下去。隐忍负重、老实忠厚的性格，由此渐居上风，一段时间内成为直隶人的主要文化性格。但隐忍老实犹如显性基因，刻于表面；任侠尚义犹如隐性基因，深藏其内。只有当异变发生，河北人隐藏的品格才会流露出来——从燕赵时代传承下来的战斗精神才能得以彰显。这就是为什么虽然历经数百年在天子脚下经受皇权规训，但每逢变乱之时，河北人的气魄和伟力总能在历史上留下浓墨重彩的一笔的原因。

当朝廷出了大奸臣，河北就出了"硬汉"杨继盛；当朝代更替、江山易手，河北就出了传奇义士孙奇逢；当维新事业受阻，河北就出了大刀王五；当时代在探索新路，河北就出了李大钊；当国家遭遇入侵，河北就出了喜峰口长城抗战，出了狼牙山五壮士，出了骨头越打越硬的英雄……燕赵多慷慨悲歌之士，历经两千多年的时光，你以为豪侠—圣贤已经成为历史的化石，殊不知它却化作一股侠气，潜藏成了河北人的精神底色：一种在外力冲击下就能随时爆发的集体无意识。

河北的历史堪称中国历史的缩小版，从古至今的文明都镌刻在这片土地上。在中国的传统观念中，一直存在着农耕文明和游牧文明的对峙，这两种文化，仿若有着天然的圈层壁垒。但事实上，任何两种事物之间，都没有鲜明的分界线，哪怕是长城，也不是一道文明意义上的分界线，长城内外两种文明的交汇与冲突时有发生。河北一直徘徊在这条线上，是两种文明的角力场，也是两种文明互相消化的胃。现在的河北，北部的承德和张家口部分地区，仍有浓厚的游牧文明气息。坝上草原、木兰围场和避暑山庄，昭示着历史上文明之间的整合。而河北中部、南部，则是中原农耕文明最为经典的组成部分。邯郸更是举国罕见的三千多年来未曾改名的城市，这或许也是文化稳定性的一个隐喻。近代以来，海洋文明兴起，河北又站立在了外来文明冲击和吸纳的第一线。秦皇岛、唐山和沧州，均位于环渤海地区，从秦皇东巡、魏武挥鞭到近现代工业崛起、海上航运兴盛，历史与现实总在某些时刻光影交错。

从历史的经验来看，河北人在和平岁月，一定是深藏不露，即便负重前行，也隐忍无言；但到了危难时刻，也一定会恢复慷慨悲歌的历史心性，彰显出豪侠圣贤的精神底色，挺身而出，震动天下。这就是河北人的文化特征与精神底色。

第2篇
自然奇观　山川之美

　　河北省地处沿海与内陆交接地带，是中国唯一兼有高原、平原、湖泊、山地、丘陵、盆地、海滨等各种地貌类型的省份，地貌景观异彩纷呈：北戴河金沙碧浪，人间胜景；嶂石岩红崖长墙，气势壮阔；崆山白云洞天堂地府，五洞连环。燕赵大地多样的地貌单元形成了各异的气候类型，为各类植物和动物提供了良好的生存和栖息地。雾灵山、野三坡，辽河源、坝上草原则是在游山赏景的同时，领略河北大地动植物资源丰盛与独特的绝佳去处。

北戴河

——碧海金沙滩，消暑绝胜地

浪淘沙·北戴河

毛泽东

大雨落幽燕，

白浪滔天，

秦皇岛外打鱼船。

一片汪洋都不见，

知向谁边？

往事越千年，

魏武挥鞭，

东临碣石有遗篇。

萧瑟秋风今又是，

换了人间。

　　北戴河是我国北方最负盛名的天然海滨浴场，海岸漫长曲折，滩面平缓，沙软潮平，海水清澈。据地下考古发现，在北戴河横山南边，近年发现并发掘了一组大型建筑群的遗址。据考证和推断，这处建筑群遗址是秦始皇东巡时的行宫，被国务院列为全国重点文物保护单位。目前，这里有一幢幢的西式别墅和中式宫殿楼阁，加上近几年兴建的一批设备齐全的宾馆、旅店，共3 000多幢。这里每年接待几百万国内游客及来自近百个国家和地区的一批批外宾、旅游者。

　　北戴河位于秦皇岛西南15千米处，北有联峰山作屏障，南临茫茫沧海。风光明媚，气候宜人，春无风沙，冬无严寒，秋季天高气爽，夏季最热的农历六七月，平均气温也只有23℃。整个风景区，东自鸽子窝、金山嘴起，西至戴河口止，长约13千米，宽约2千米，为一条狭长的沿海地带。这里沙软潮平，是海水浴的好地方。翠黛的山峦、明净的海滩、幽静的别墅、优美的园林，把海边长廊装点得绚丽多彩。盛夏时节，游客来到北戴河便会陶醉在迷人的海滨风光之中，清晨看日出，午间洗海澡，傍晚观海潮，待到明月高悬，漫步在沙滩上，欣赏那松涛海涛汇成的美妙交响乐，令人心旷神怡。这里是中国著名的风景区，也是驰名中外的避暑、疗养胜地，被列为国家级风景名胜区。

北戴河景点主要有联峰山、碧螺塔、鸽子窝、老虎石等，这些名胜都各有情趣，引人入胜。这儿的山格外青，海也格外蓝。常常一天之内就可以观赏到许多景致：日出日落，涨潮落潮，风和阴晴，真是变幻多姿，各有佳妙。

联峰山公园又称莲蓬山公园。位于北戴河海滨中心偏西，东西横亘 5 千米，由东联峰、中联峰和西联峰山呈南北纵向排列。三座被松林覆盖的山峰，因山势连缀故有联峰之称，远视又似莲蓬，亦称为莲蓬山。1919 年建成北戴河最大的森林公园，以登山览胜和林中探幽为特点。最高峰东联峰山海拔 153 米，是北戴河的制高点。游人观景登高主要以东联峰山为主。山顶建有望海亭，登亭远眺，北戴河海滨的秀丽风光尽收眼底。各式楼房别墅，掩映在松涛之中，别有情趣。近年，在中联峰山主峰绝顶发现了"汉武台"，联峰山神秘的面纱正在逐步被揭开。联峰山景区，山海相映，花木繁茂，幽雅恬静，山峦俊秀，林深谷幽，奇石怪洞，比比皆是。古今游人多有吟咏，令人流连忘返。

碧螺塔公园，位于北戴河海滨小东山，这里三面环海，风光绚丽。碧螺塔为公园的主景建筑，它是以世界独一无二的仿海螺形状建造的螺旋观光塔，为海滨东山地区的最

鸽子窝公园

高点。登塔远眺，一望无际，茫茫大海尽收眼底，使人心旷神怡。碧螺塔周围，礁石林立，因适宜浮游生物生长，所以各种鱼、蟹、贝类等海洋生物资源极为丰富，是垂钓的天然宝地。一代伟人邓小平曾多次来此休闲垂钓。半岛上设有"邓小平垂钓处"纪念碑。为了缅怀一代伟人，公园于 2003 年建立了"碧螺塔海上垂钓基地"，每年 9 月至 10 月举办"北戴河海上垂钓节"。园内备有大小船只五十余艘及多种渔具、网具，可供游客岸边、近海及深海垂钓。

鸽子窝公园，位于北戴河海滨的最东端，占地 300 余亩，是观赏海上日出的最佳之处。在因断裂所形成的临海悬崖上，屹立着形似雄鹰的鹰角石，通高 20 余米，过去常有成群的鸽子或朝暮相聚或筑巢于石缝之中，因此得名鸽子窝。每逢夏日清晨，这里云集数万名游客观赏"红日浴海"的奇景。漫步在 182 米长的望海长廊上任由海风吹拂，在碧湖之畔樱花树下静坐看白鸟飞舞，清静雅致，怡然自得。

老虎石海上公园，位于北戴河风景区中心，占地总面积 3.3 万平方米，公园内形态不一的各种礁石，状似群虎。这里滩宽海阔，入海坡度平缓，水质良好，因而成为暑期海浴人数最多的浴场。这里还有大型的娱乐公园，内设有海上飞伞、帆板、冲浪板、儿童乐园等，是目前国内较大的海上综合性公园。老虎石西，有 1957 年经朱德同志特批兴建的小码头，可停泊小型游艇、游船，是观景、垂钓的理想之地。小码头西有"望龟亭"一座，小巧玲珑，颇具情趣。

北戴河的鸟类资源极为丰富，据有关资料记载，我国鸟类共计 1 186 种，而北戴河就有 20 目 61 科 405 种。其中属国家重点保护动物的 68 种，不少还是世界著名的珍禽。早在 20 世纪初，就有美国、德国等鸟类学者前来考察鸟类资源并写有专著。近年来，英国、美国、日本、丹麦、比利时、澳大利亚等国的众多鸟类科研工作者和鸟类爱好者接踵而至，进行学术研究和观鸟活动。专家认为北戴河是最好的观鸟和鸟类研究的基地之一。

第7章

雾灵山

——求道灵山，避暑凉岛

雾灵山是燕山山脉主峰，位于河北省兴隆县，被誉为"华北物种基因库"，保留有良好的原始森林景象。

顾炎武在其《昌平山水记》中说："其山高峻，有云雾蒙其上，四时不绝。"这可能就是雾灵山得名的原因。

雾灵山作为求道名山始于宋代，当时已修建了诸多庙宇，"有僧道万余人"。元代曾有僧道来此做佛事，《昌平山水记》中记载："（元）文宗命西僧于雾灵山作佛事一月。"现存的寺庙遗址有红梅寺、钟古院、云峰寺等，在当时被称为下院、中院和上院。相传

雾灵山

过去在红梅寺"有名和尚三千六，无名和尚赛牛毛"，可见求道名山名不虚传。明洪武年间，中丞刘基（字伯温）巡视边陲重镇曹家路时，曾登临雾灵山，行至半山劳累烦热，歇脚于一巨石下，忽觉一阵凉风袭来，疲劳顿觉消失，遂题写"雾灵山清凉界"六个大字。200年后的明崇祯八年（1635年），后人在此石上刻字铭古，成为京东特有的石质巨碑，人称"大字石"，上刻有"雾灵山清凉界"六个大字，每字约4平方米，豪放洒脱，苍劲有力。清顺治二年（1645年）雾灵山被划为清东陵的"后龙风水禁地"，封禁长达270年。清圣祖康熙帝在《晓发古北口望雾灵山》中写道："流吹凌晨发，长旍出塞分。远峰犹见月，古木半笼云。地迥疏人迹，山回簇马群。观风当夏景，涧草自含薰。"雾灵山在清代长期的封禁下，给森林的生长和野生动物的繁衍创造了条件，雾灵山形成了"森林满山、树木遮天、野兽无数、遍地涌泉"的壮丽景观。

新中国成立之后，为了保护这块绿色宝地，成立了专门的机构，建设和经营雾灵山这片宝贵的森林，才有了我们今天看到的雾灵山的面貌。

1988年经国务院批准建立的雾灵山国家级自然保护区是河北省第一个国家级自然保护区。总面积1.5万公顷，保护对象为"温带森林生态系统和猕猴分布北限"。温带森林生态系统是指雾灵山位于蒙古、东北、华北三大植物区系交会处，各种植物成分兼而有之，生态系统复杂多样，成为温带生物多样性的保留地和生物资源宝库。猕猴分布北限是指

雾灵山中的猕猴

雾灵山以北，世界上再也没有野生灵长类生存了。雾灵山不仅是猕猴分布北限，而且还是南北动物的走廊和许多南方动物的分布北限，如勺鸡、果子狸等，同时，还是许多北方代表动物的分布南限，如花尾榛鸡、攀雀等。截至 2022 年 4 月 30 日，雾灵山有高等植物 168 科 665 属 1 870 种，其中国家一级保护植物有人参，二级保护植物有核桃，三级保护植物有核桃楸、野大豆、青檀等 8 种。有陆生脊椎动物 173 种，其中一级保护动物有金雕、金钱豹 2 种，二级保护动物有秃鹫、猫猴、斑羚等 15 种，雾灵山这座活的自然博物馆可让大家一饱眼福。

森林覆盖率高达 93% 的雾灵山国家级自然保护区以森林景观为主体，苍山奇峰为骨架，清溪碧潭为脉络，文物古迹点缀其间，构成了一幅静态景观与动态景观相协调、自然景观与人文景观浑然一体、风格独特的生动画卷。这里山峦重叠，恬静瑰丽，曲流溪涧，晶莹碧透，烟雾浩渺，如梦似幻，奇峰怪石，如雕如塑。春天，万物复苏，鸟语花香，花红柳绿，蜂蝶缠绕，杜鹃花、丁香花、忍冬花等竞相开放，姹紫嫣红，即使是绿色，也显出浓淡不同的色彩和层次。夏日，山外骄阳似火，山内则树木葱郁，金莲花如金铺地，银莲花似玉漫坡，凉风送爽，飞瀑流泉，潭幽溪清。秋天，山下一片翠绿，山上的桦树、落叶松已变成金黄，山腰的山杨、五角枫、栋树，一层层地变黄、变红、变紫。放眼望去，片片红叶，串串硕果，点点簇簇地镶嵌在峰岭层叠之间，似碧波上漂浮的片片红帆，又似蓝天上飘荡的朵朵霞云。冬天，崇山峻岭，银装素裹，玉树琼花，茫茫林海一派北国风光，苍松翠柏雪中刚劲挺拔，幽韵清冷，更显出雾灵山凛然飘逸的冷峻神态。

第 8 章
野三坡
——华北峡谷珍品

　　野三坡国家地质公园主要由冲蚀嶂谷、断裂峡谷、岩溶洞泉和森林景观组成。在大地构造上，野三坡处于太行山断裂隆起带和燕山皱褶带接合部。冲蚀嶂谷是垂直裂隙和节理发育而成的可溶性岩体，经流水长期冲刷和溶蚀所形成的峡谷地貌。

　　作为国家重点风景名胜区和国家 5A 级旅游景区的野三坡，共由 100 多个景点和功能各异的 7 个景区构成，包括百里峡自然风景游览区、拒马河避暑疗养游乐区、白草畔原始森林保护区、鱼谷洞奇泉怪洞游览区、龙门天关长城文物保护区、金华山灵奇狩游乐区、野三坡失乐园熏衣草主题庄园。

　　"天下第一峡"的百里峡，是野三坡的王牌景点，几乎所有到野三坡旅游的人都会去体验它的雄伟、险峻、神奇和幽深。峡谷内奇岩耸立、绝壁万仞、草木横生，千奇百怪的岩溶壮景集雄、险、奇、幽为一体，构成一幅浓墨重彩的大自然"百里画廊"。百里峡之所以能有如此神奇的魅力，主要得益于百里峡的冲蚀嶂谷地貌类型。峡谷两侧多为冲天绝壁，直上直下，谷壁与谷底近乎垂直，如刀削斧劈一般，谷底有少量沉积物。

　　百里峡中蕴藏着丰富的地貌和地质科学知识。景点"蛙蟹斗智"，是形似青蛙、螃蟹的三块巨石，其学名叫作"崩塌岩块"，其成因是岩层垂直裂隙发育，受到震动或重力的作用，岩壁上的岩块崩落，形成了这种特殊的灾害地质遗迹。景点"一线天"，代表的则是嶂谷形成的初级阶段，在物理风化作用和间歇性山洪下切及侧向侵蚀下，垂直地面的裂隙不断扩张，从而形成了狭窄的嶂谷。嶂谷两侧岩壁上的钟乳石，学名为"近代钙华"，是岩石中的碳酸钙溶解沉积的结果。道路中央具有波浪痕迹的扁平大石，则记录了 10 亿年前湖滨和海岸地区的波浪在松散未固结的沉积物表面留下的痕迹。景点"金线悬针"则是大自然带给人们的又一个惊喜，在山体又深又窄的岩壁裂缝中，夹着一块巨大的岩石，好似一根穿在线上的针。据地质专家研究，亿万年前由于地质运动或地震发生的一瞬，从山顶震落的岩石在下坠过程中由于裂开的山体再度复合上，坠石被卡在当中而形成这一奇观。

　　可以说，百里峡就是一部天然的地质教科书，各种地质奇观在这里竞相比美。石雕观音是花岗岩在大自然的雕琢下形成的杰作。由于岩石中发育了许多组垂直裂隙，在垮塌过程中形成岩柱，再经过长期的球状风化后形成了今天我们看到的观音的头和脖子。离石雕观音很近的虎泉，则是典型的裂隙泉，其成因是岩层中发育了很多裂隙，裂隙中的水向下渗透和汇聚，遇到下方的不透水岩层阻挡后水无法下渗，而出露成泉。百里峡中的天然石拱桥——天成桥，桥长 10 米，宽 2 米，厚 1.5 米，桥孔高 11 米，桥墩由 6 500 万年前的侵入岩浆岩所构成，桥梁则是 10 亿年前的沉积白云岩。在白云岩形成以后，距今 6 500 万年前时发生了岩浆侵入，岩浆侵入冷凝后形成现在的岩浆岩桥墩，由于白云岩中发育了多组方向的裂隙，在距今 70 万年前左右，地壳抬升，经物理风化，白云岩开始沿裂隙和节理面层层剥落，又经流水冲刷侵蚀，形成了今天桥墩和桥梁分别由岩浆岩和白云岩两种岩石构成的天生桥。

在百里峡这个大自然的杰作中，人们不仅能欣赏到瑰丽的美景，更能获得意料之外的地理和地质知识。当人们在游览过程中仔细驻足观看不同地质景观的详细说明时，就会感受到大自然真实的美。

百里峡一线天

拒马河自东向西流经野三坡 70 余里，两岸群峰崛立，怪石峥嵘，河水潺潺，清可照人。游人既可中流泛舟，饱览山光水色，亦可击水畅游，领略大自然的情趣。洁白松软的沙丘是沙浴、日光浴的理想场地。度假村、苗寨与四周景点浑然一体，是休闲、娱乐、避暑的最佳选择。

龙门天关景区山峰挺拔，断崖绝壁高耸入云，山谷中清泉溪流激浪奔腾，景色尤为壮观。自古以来，这里都是京都通往紫荆关的交通要道和兵家必争之地，金、明、清各代都把此地视为军事要塞，派重兵把守。所以，景区内有许多文物名胜遗留至今，现有的"大龙门城堡""蔡树庵长城""摩崖石刻"等都是河北省重点文物保护单位。

龙门峡峡谷幽深，山峰耸立，气势磅礴。这里的燕山构造期花岗岩所构成的地貌，奇特而美丽，天犬待月、神狮峰、天师讲箕鱼鳞石、千层石等，栩栩如生。著名的紫荆关深断裂切穿花岗岩体，形成龙门天关陡崖绝壁。沿天沟断层峡谷而上，可看到断裂发生时留下的断层破碎带、断层擦痕、镜面等断层痕迹。由于花岗岩中多组节理发育，经长期风化侵蚀后形成多级陡坎，多阶瀑布尽汇清潭，翠碧尽染，美如天庭。

在野三坡的东面和东南面，是灰岩和白云岩，每一层岩石都含有它形成期间的海生动物化石。如果你有机会到野三坡走一走，并留心看一看暴露出来的岩层，你还会注意到，岩层并不平整，大多呈褶曲状。这是因为地层形成之初，当地地壳以下沉为主，接受了各种物质的沉积；后期转化为上升，巨厚的沉积物受到挤压而发生褶皱。此外，这里的许多岩石表面还有有规律的"波痕"，这是岩石形成之时波浪在松软沉积物表面留下的痕迹。

白草畔森林游览区是野三坡的制高点，海拔 1 983 米，这里山势挺拔，奇峰怪石林立，满山野花盛开，野生动物成群，森林遮天蔽日堪称太行"绿色明珠"。登石城岭可观日出赏云海，探蚂蚁岭上的红蚁巢穴，听风动石畔的松涛，赏千亩杜鹃，游万亩林海，使人流连忘返。

第9章
嶂石岩
——三栈牟九套，四屏藏八景

八百里太行山，在河北来说，不是因为它的高度令人向往，而是那种在水平方向上横向展开的魅力，横向展开的那一面犹如万里长城般的山崖随时震撼着人心。在大自然的演变中，太行山形成了一种别样的地质地貌，其中最具代表性的就是和喀斯特地貌、丹霞地貌齐名的嶂石岩地貌。

在距离省会石家庄 100 千米左右的赞皇县嶂石岩纸糊套景区，最为知名的便是嶂石岩的标志性景观——赤壁丹崖。这面横亘眼前的红色崖壁已矗立千万年，在晨光下，崖

清晨的嶂石岩

壁的色彩由深到浅不断变幻，先是绚烂的红，而后变成鲜亮的黄，最后逐渐恢复成普通日光下的灰。"岩半花宫千仞余，遥观疑是挂空虚。丹屏翠碧相辉映，纵有王维画不如"的风光，曾引发无数赞叹。

嶂石岩展示了太行山的高亢、粗犷、奇险、含蓄和雄浑，万丈红绫的高度、广度和深度组成的三维空间与云雾、绿植结合，让嶂石岩在视觉上产生了蒙太奇的幻境。

原本声名不显的嶂石岩，被人们发现和认识，源于一次地质考察。1972年，河北地理所研究员郭康在太行山考察中发现了一种气势壮阔的红崖长墙砂岩地貌，后经多年考察研究，正式将该地貌命名为嶂石岩地貌。嶂石岩地貌为中国三大景观砂岩地貌（其余两个为丹霞地貌、张家界地貌）之一，是太行山雄险、壮美的典型代表地段，这种地貌有五大特点：丹崖长墙连续不断、阶梯状陡崖贯穿全境、"Ω"形嶂谷相连成套、棱角鲜明的块状结构、沟谷垂直自始至终，并蕴藏着大量奇特的地质、地貌景观，和与之相关的"天人合一"的历史与地方文化景观。

嶂石岩位处太行山中段，在地质构造上属于轴向呈南北且向北倾斜的赞皇大背斜西翼，其组成主要为中元古代长城纪砂岩，上面覆盖着古生代寒武纪灰岩，构成了太行山的主脊。由于地层产状比较平缓，垂直裂隙比较发育，厚层砂岩中夹有薄层黏土岩，块体崩塌与侵蚀、剥蚀比较盛行，导致地势异常险峻，造景地貌比较齐全，景色蔚为壮观，因而被命名为嶂石岩地貌。

嶂石岩景观主要为丹崖、壁岭、奇峰、幽谷，其景观特色大致可概括为"三栈牵九套，四屏藏八景"，三栈即三条古道，九套即连接三条古道的九条山谷，四屏乃整体看似四道屏障而又相对独立的四个景区（九女峰、圆通寺、纸糊套、冻凌背），这四个景区中有八处著名胜景：九仙聚会、岩半花宫、晴天飞雨、回音巨崖、淮泉凉意、冻凌玉柱、重门锁翠、叠嶂悬钟。这三栈四屏、八景九套之间均有小路相连，将120个景点连珠缀串，迤逦展开。其中回音巨崖、冻凌玉柱、雾洞、佛光为"嶂岩四绝"；晴天飞雨、石乳灵泉、云崖撒珠、银瀑落湖又作"嶂岩水景四绝"。

当你穿梭在嶂石岩那令人神往的名胜和景点中，固然是一番亲近大自然的滋味。要领略嶂石岩的美，就要知道嶂石岩的美是如何形成的。只有掌握了更多关于嶂石岩的知识，才能真正认识嶂石岩所展示的大自然最为神奇的一面。

嶂石岩的万丈红绫，地质学上称为"长崖"，是山地夷平面被切割破坏的产物，也有的是由断裂形成。长崖经过自然的切割和破坏，往往会形成长几十米至几百米、高数十米甚至上百米、两面陡直壁立的山体，形如一堵大墙，故而称为断墙。在冻凌背景区以北这种地质特征尤为明显。由长崖到断墙是一个变化发育过程，随着时间的流逝、地质的变迁，断墙被进一步分割破坏，形成方山、台柱、塔峰等地质景观。以方山为例，景区内的黄庵垴就是典型；以塔峰为例，景区内的九女峰就是典型。人们在嶂石岩景区看到的红色长崖，主要是由红色石英岩组成且一侧基岩裸露的陡崖，它由三层叠置的长崖组成，三层长崖之间是两级平台，当地人称之为"栈"。台面上堆积着崩落下来的大小石块，石块间长满了灌木和草丛。盛夏时节，犹如两条碧玉腰带缠绕在长崖之间，使得长崖更加壮观、秀美。

如果说以长崖为代表的景观是嶂石岩的一副面孔的话，那么独特的连环成套的"Ω"形嶂谷则是嶂石岩展现给世人的另一副面孔。"Ω"形嶂谷的典型代表就是 1997 年被收入吉尼斯世界纪录的回音壁。回音壁又称回音崖，位于嶂石岩景区内的回音谷。其造型为半圆形，如"Ω"，半圆直径达 90 米，弧度 250 度，弧长 300 米。站在山谷的任一地方说话，反射回来的声音都异常清晰，空谷悠扬，清音透亮，满山都回荡着此起彼伏的声音。

嶂石岩是太行山的精华，是太行山的一颗璀璨明珠，观太行，必去嶂石岩，了解过后，确实令人心之向往。

第10章
衡水湖
——燕赵最美湿地，鸟类天堂

　　"一湖蒹葭一湖花，一湖鸥鹭一湖鸭。"

　　每年的 10 月份，享有东亚地区蓝宝石、京津冀最美湿地、京南第一湖众多美誉的衡水湖，正处在最清爽、舒畅的季节。

　　河北衡水湖国家级自然保护区位于华北平原中南部的衡水市冀州区城区北侧，是河北省著名的湖泊湿地，这里有宽广的湖水、茂密的芦苇荡，还有荷塘、湖心岛。总面积 187.87 平方千米。其生物多样性十分丰富，以内陆淡水湿地生态系统和国家一级、二级鸟类为主要保护对象。高贵的仙鹤、美丽的天鹅、灵巧的鸥鸟、轻盈的白鹭，翩翩起舞、悠然嬉戏。

　　公元前 602 年，黄河决口改道，冲刷形成了这一片洼地，因常年积水，史称"千顷洼"，面积 120 平方千米，其中深水面积 19 平方千米，碧波荡漾、渔歌唱晚，素有"北方江南"

衡水湖中的水鸟

之称。其水源主要来自卫运河、黄河和长江水，可谓"容长江、黄河于一湖——衡水湖"。

衡水湖自然保护区属暖温带大陆季风气候区，四季分明，年平均气温 13.0℃，年降雨量 518.9 毫米。优越的自然环境非常适宜野生动植物的生存和繁衍。区内有植物 370 种，昆虫 194 种，鱼类 26 种，两栖爬行类 17 种，鸟类 296 种，兽类 17 种，浮游植物 201 种，浮游动物 174 种，底栖动物 23 种。在众多的野生动植物中，尤为突出的是鸟类资源，国家一级重点保护的有丹顶鹤、白鹤、黑鹳、东方白鹳、大鸨、金雕、白肩雕 7 种，国家二级重点保护的鸟类有大天鹅、小天鹅、灰鹤等 44 种。每年在这里营巢繁殖的夏候鸟有数十万只，以须浮鸥、黑翅长脚鹬等鸟类为主，越冬的灰鹤有 3 000 多只，雁类上万只，遮天蔽日的灰椋鸟更形成了一道蔚为壮观的风景线。

衡水湖具有蓄洪防涝防旱、调节气候、控制土壤侵蚀、降解环境污染等功能，它不但造福衡水人民，而且对调节周边乃至京津地区的气候、改善生态环境起到重要作用，它还是南水北调的调蓄水源地，为衡水及周边地市提供饮用水和工农业用水，发挥着促进区域经济发展的重要作用，其生态效益、社会效益、经济效益巨大。

衡水湖自然保护区位于环京津经济圈、环渤海经济圈、黄河经济协作区和东北亚经济圈之中，处于方圆 300 千米以内的北京和天津两个直辖市，石家庄、太原、郑州、济南四个省会城市，26 个地级市的假日经济圈之内。其明显的区位优势、独特的湿地资源、优美怡人的自然风光和悠久的历史文化，具有开展生态旅游得天独厚的先决条件。为此，按照保护—开发利用—保护良性循环的原则，以保护生物多样性为核心，以生态科普旅游为特色，以实现自然资源可持续利用和经济的可持续发展为目标，将通过实施衡水湖西湖、滏阳新河滩地恢复湿地，利用南水北调，开辟新水域，扩大湿地面积，周边建设水源涵养林、改善生态环境，挖掘开发历史人文资源、加快生态旅游基础设施、生态服务区建设，加大核心区、缓冲区生物多样性保护力度，促进实验区和示范区生态科普旅游业及相关产业的发展，使衡水湖自然保护区成为一个环境优美、资源保护、居民乐业、经济发达的国家级自然保护区，成为具有湿地保护和经济发展、实现自然资源可持续利用的国内外湿地保护的示范区。

衡水湖自然保护区不仅生物多样性丰富、自然风光优美，而且文化底蕴丰厚，源远流长。位于衡水湖南岸的冀州古城建于汉高祖六年（公元前 201 年），史有"天下分九州，冀州为首"之称。汉城墙、明城墙、众多汉代古墓、石碑、李三娘石磨及竹林寺飞升上天的许多传说再现了衡水湖的自然、历史、人文景观，让人无不感慨衡水湖的神奇与秀美。

第11章

坝上草原

——草的世界，花的海洋

　　"坝上"是一地理名词，特指由草原陡然升高而形成的地带，又因气候和植被的原因形成的草甸式草原。现泛指张家口和承德以北100千米处，统称为坝上地区，包括张家口坝上的张北、尚义、康保、沽源四县，承德坝上的丰宁、围场两县，以及内蒙古的克什克腾旗和多伦县。总面积二十多万平方千米。

　　坝上地区就旅游地域而言，主要分为围场坝上（木兰围场）、丰宁坝上、张北坝上和沽源坝上等区域，是内蒙古高原的重要组成部分，其中木兰围场—乌兰布统大草原最为美丽，但距离北京也最远。坝上草原总面积约350平方千米，是内蒙古草原的一部分；尤其紧挨内蒙古的康保草原最具内蒙古草原风格。平均海拔1 486米，最高海拔约2 400米；是滦河、潮河的发源地。夏季，这里天蓝欲滴，碧草如翠，云花清秀，野芳琼香，置身于草青云淡、繁花遍野的茫茫碧野中，天穹压落、云欲擦肩；金秋时节，万山红遍，野果飘香；冬季，白雪皑皑，玉树琼花。

承德市围场满族蒙古族自治县御道口草原

坝上地形为丘岭、平原,东南高、西北低;河网密布,水淖丰富。

坝上草地为高原草场,海拔在 1 200～1 400 米之间,沿坝有许多关口和山峰,最高在海拔 2 500 米以上,是坝上高原的重要组成部分,典型的干旱型草原,当地人叫草滩。草原旱禾草居多,草层高度为 15～40 厘米。这类草原占坝上草原大部分。草甸草原是草原中最好的一类,主要植物为多年生草本植物,高度约 30～60 厘米,有各种野花盛开其间。沽源的五花草甸、闪电河畔、察北牧场,围场的大部分地区,丰宁大滩部分地区多见这类草原。这里洼水清澈,青草齐肩,黄羊成群,生态环境优良。蒙古语称此地为"海留图",意为水草丰茂的地方。

坝上天高气爽,芳草如茵,骏马壮硕,牛羊如云;坝缘山峰如簇,碧水潺潺;接坝区域森林茂密,山珍遍野,野味无穷;上坝后,即可给你怡人的消暑之感。凉风拂面掠过,顷刻间钻进你的衣襟。环顾四野,在茂密的绿草甸子上,点缀着繁星般的野花。大片大片的白桦林,浓妆玉肌,层层叠叠的枝叶间,漏下斑斑点点的日影。美丽的闪电河如玉带环绕,静静地流过你的身边。牛群、马群、羊群群栖觅食,放牧人粗犷的歌声和清脆的长鞭声,融合着悦耳动听的鸟声,更给朴实的草原增添了无限的生机。

坝上天然林主要分布在围场塞罕坝一带、沽源东南部、丰宁沿坝一带。天然林多以白桦、山杨、杏林为主;灌木林有白榆、小红柳、沙杞柳、柠条等;人工林坝上东部以松树为主,西部以杨树为主。森林覆盖率从 8%～12% 不等,尤其是围场已达 30% 到 70% 以上,是国家森林公园所在地。这里生态环境较好。西部一般是荒漠特征,人工林较多。坝上树木的多少,直接影响到北京周边生态环境。坝上河流多为内流河,季节性强,经常干涸。雨季山洪、河流聚到一处,形成"淖",最大的淖在尚义、张北境内,称"察汗淖、安固里淖"。最大的外流河是滦河,发源于丰宁、流经沽源称"闪电河",正蓝旗称"上都河",入多伦后复经丰宁、围场向南称"滦河"。

坝上天然淖、水库多达上百个,较大的有尚义的察汗淖、张北的安固里淖、黄盖淖,沽源的闪电河水库、丰宁的湿地,围场的月亮湖、将军泡子。这些水域里都生长有天然鱼,以鲫鱼、鲤鱼为多,水库和淖周围多是湿地,水草丰美,天鹅、地鹊多见。

坝上属大陆性季风气候,年均气温 1～2℃,无霜期 90～120 天,年降水量 400 毫米左右。寒冷、多风、干旱是坝上最明显的特征。旅游季节平均气温为 17.4℃,是理想的绿色健康旅游休闲胜地。夏季无暑,清新宜人。斑斓的野花,始于坝缘,有的灿若金星,有的纤若红簪,四季花色各异,早晚浓淡分明。夜幕之时,明月篝火,是诉说情话的好去处;可以到篝火旁同南来北往的游客尽情地攀谈、跳舞、唱歌;还可以独自坐在草原上,享受独处的妙趣。清晨起床,你可以踏着软软的天然草毡,聆听百鸟清脆的歌声;也可去看看草原的日出。一轮红日冉冉升起,绿叶上晶莹透明的露珠,立刻变成了闪烁的珍珠;各种植物转眼一片嫩绿;马群、牛群、羊群也在广阔的草原上开始蠕动,真是一片"天苍苍、野茫茫,风吹草低见牛羊"的草原胜景。

第3篇
古城古韵　名城之美

城市，承载了历史的遗存，见证了尘世的沧桑，是生活在那里的人们千百年的创造，是厚重的历史和文化不朽的结晶。阅读城市，留住那份文化记忆。对河北而言，这里有承德、保定、正定、山海关、邯郸、蔚县6座国家级历史文化名城，也有宣化、涿州、定州、赵县、邢台、大名6座省级历史文化名城。一座座文化名城如一颗颗明珠点缀于燕赵大地之上，以其独特的魅力吸引着世界各地的游人，向世人讲述着这片热土悠久的历史和璀璨的文化。

第 12 章

承德

——清代皇家的避暑围猎之地

　　承德，旧称"热河"，处于华北和东北两个地区的连接过渡地带。地近京津，背靠蒙辽，省内与秦皇岛、唐山两个沿海城市以及张家口市相邻，是首批 24 个国家级历史文化名城之一、中国十大风景名胜之一、旅游胜地四十佳之一、国家重点风景名胜区，是国家甲类开放城市。1994 年位于承德市的避暑山庄及其周围寺庙被联合国教科文组织批准为世界文化遗产，从而使承德步入世界文化名城的行列。2012 年，承德被评为中国"十大特色休闲城市"之一。

　　承德有深厚的地域文化底蕴。"红山文化"是承德新石器时期的历史文化遗迹，距今已经有 5 000 多年。在新石器时代后期氏族社会转化时，即游牧民族从蒙古高原沿河流进入平原区过渡到农耕生活，都曾在热河地带经过，这里是人类进化、发展的折转区域。这一时期被称为燕山文化，与燕赵文化一起成为河北的历史主体文化。

　　春秋战国时代，承德一带隶属于燕国设置的渔阳、右北平、辽西三郡。《史记·匈奴传》记载，燕国曾在这一带修筑长城，现在古长城遗址，仍旧依稀可见。著名的兴隆农具铁范的发现，说明当时这一带的农业生产已经相当发达。秦汉以后，历代的中央政权都曾在此设置过行政管理机构。在漫长的封建社会历史中，这里的汉、匈奴、乌桓、鲜卑、库莫奚、契丹、突厥、蒙古等各民族的经济文化得到进一步发展。

　　清朝建立后，我国统一的多民族国家政权进一步巩固。在当时的历史条件下，热河的地理位置日益重要，这里毗邻京、津，西顾张家口，东接辽宁，北倚内蒙古，南邻唐山，是燕山腹地、渤海之滨的重要区域性城市。由于这里的气候、物产等自然条件得天独厚，既可消夏避暑，又可联络蒙古，巩固边防。于是清朝从康熙四十二年（1703 年）开始兴建避暑山庄，直至乾隆五十七年（1792 年）工程才告结束。避暑山庄建立后，清朝曾有 7 个皇帝在此驻跸。在 150 多年的时间里，避暑山庄经历了兴盛、衰败、复兴的曲折发展过程。清代康乾年间，是避暑山庄和外八庙的兴盛时期。帝王们在此消夏理政，使这里成为全国的第二个政治中心。随着清王朝的国势衰弱，鼎盛一时的避暑山庄和外八庙开始败落。

承德双塔山

承德作为清代皇家重要活动地，汇集过王朝的各民族王公大臣，现存有中国三大古建筑群之一的避暑山庄和外八庙。1976 年，国务院批准了《避暑山庄和外八庙整修工程第一个十年规划》，避暑山庄和外八庙得以大规模整修。

承德古城是集皇家文化、古建筑文化、佛教文化和中原儒家文化于一体的中国历史文化名城。承德的国家级重点保护文物除避暑山庄和外八庙之外，还有城隍庙和金山岭长城等地。

承德城隍庙即乾隆钦定"热河都城隍庙"，位于承德市中心，西大街路北，距避暑山庄约 1 千米。这是一座典型的汉式寺庙，格局简练。城隍庙黄琉璃覆顶，彩饰飞扬，有意无意地显示出它傲然于各地城隍庙的尊贵。现内设神像近 90 座，主体建筑福荫严疆殿供奉着一尊城隍坐像，面目慈善，号称"天下第一城隍"。传说城隍神是康熙皇帝十七皇子允礼。允礼自幼豁达识体，不参与皇权之争，且又聪明持重，政绩斐然。他死后，乾隆帝深感若失股肱。乾隆三十七年（1772 年）值工部尚书周元理奏请修建热河都城隍庙，乾隆下旨拨款施工，封允礼为热河城隍神。除"天下第一城隍"外，其余各殿供奉文、武、义、财神、孔子、朱熹、文昌帝君和极具特色的六十甲子神。

金山岭长城是明代修筑的一段长城。它横亘在河北省滦平县与北京市密云区交界地带的燕山支脉，西起历史上著名的古北口关口，东至高耸入云的望京楼，全长 10.5 千米，沿线设有大小关隘5处，敌楼67座，烽燧2座，因其视野开阔，敌楼密集，景观奇特，建筑艺术精美，军事防御体系健全，保存完好而著称于世。此外还有奇特的景观：仙山琼阁"望京楼"、惊险奇观"瘦驴脊"、高耸云天"登天梯"、举世称奇"文字墙"、温泉、天泉、龟石、通天洞、大小金山楼等奇观异景美不胜收。金山岭长城堪称我国万里长城的精粹，比起名闻中外的八达岭长城，有过之而无不及，是一个不可多得的旅游胜地。

金山岭长城在1987年被列为世界文化遗产，为全国重点文物保护单位、国家级风景名胜区、国家4A级旅游景区。

木兰围场又称塞罕坝森林公园。塞罕坝全称塞罕达巴罕色钦，蒙语的意思是"有河源的美丽的高岭"。1681年清康熙帝为训练军队，在这里开辟了10 000多平方千米的狩猎场。清朝前半叶，皇帝每年都要率王公大臣、八旗精兵来这里举行以射猎和旅游为主的活动，史称"木兰秋狝"。

第13章
保定
——首都北京的南大门

"保定"一词，最早出现在《诗经》中《小雅·天保》一文，为"保佑安定"之意，可谓古人对美好生活的一种期盼与向往。

西有太行山屏障，东有沼泽白洋淀，易守难攻的保定，因"北控三关，南达九省，地连四部，雄冠中州"的地理位置，一直是兵家必争之地。北宋为加强北部边防，在清

直隶总督衙署

苑县（今保定市清苑区）设置保塞军，有保卫边塞之意。北宋淳化三年（992 年），建立保州城，正式开启保定千年州城的历史。

历史滚滚向前，元太祖二十二年（1227 年），成吉思汗手下大将张柔（今保定市定兴县人）"划市井，定居民，引水入城，恢复保州"，奠定了今日"靴城"的城市格局。

1272 年，元朝定都大都（今北京），在奠定今日北京城市基本格局的同时，其政治影响力也向周边辐射。曾经仅有军事功能的保州城被改为顺天路治所，并开始增加政治功能。1275 年，顺天路改名保定路，作为大都南大门，"保卫大都，安定天下"的寓意，或肇始于此。

明朝初期，将保定路改设为保定府。期间最大的变化是，为适应防御的需要，保定城由过去的土筑城墙变成砖砌城墙。明崇祯十一年（1638 年）设保定总督，辖保定、山东、天津、登莱四巡抚之地，后又增辖湖广部分地区，可谓大权在握。

清朝有 9 位总督级别的封疆大吏，号称"九大总督"，其中直隶总督管辖直隶省。由于直隶省地处京畿要地，使得直隶总督的权势很重。直隶总督的管辖区域，大致相当于今天的天津市，以及河北省大部分、河南省和山东省的小部分。

"一座总督衙署，半部清史写照"，既彰显了直隶总督的权柄，也成为直隶省会保定的繁盛见证。有"东方俾斯麦"之称的李鸿章，在平均任期 2.5 年的直隶总督任上，一干就是 25 年，身兼东宫三师、文华殿大学士、北洋通商大臣，权倾朝野。作为"九督之首"的驻地，保定政治、经济、文化等方面也随之飞跃发展。

保定府始建于 600 多年前明洪武年间，现今国内保存得最完整的省级衙署——直隶总督署坐落于古城中心，名列全国十大名园的古莲花池就在近旁。始建于元代的大慈阁，为上谷八景之一。肃穆壮观的易县清西陵、古老凝重的满城汉墓、透着慷慨悲歌之气的古易水和战国燕下都遗址、远去了鼓角铮鸣的雄县宋代地下战道遗址、显示着中华民族浩然正气的冉庄地道战遗址和狼牙山五壮士纪念塔等数不胜数的自然景观和人文景观，形成了异彩纷呈的保定旅游区域特色。

古莲花池地处河北保定市闹市区，是上谷八景之一，称"涟漪夏艳"。古莲花池是国家级文物保护单位，全国十大名园之一。始建于唐高宗年间，后经元、明重修扩建，雍正十一年（1733 年），直隶总督李卫奉旨在莲花池开办书院，一时间人才济济，扬名中外。后又辟为皇帝的行宫，乾隆、嘉庆、慈禧等帝后出巡，途经保定均在此驻跸。

大慈阁位于保定市裕华西路，与古莲花池紧邻，是历史文化名城保定的古建筑代表作和古城保定的象征，有"不到大慈阁，何曾到保定"之说。大慈阁由元代蔡国公张柔创建，原名大悲阁，位居上谷八景之首，史称"市阁凌霄"。大慈阁通高 31 米，阁前是 22 级台阶，移目阁内，观音菩萨矗立于莲瓣须弥座上，神态安然。观音像为木雕，高 5.5 米，42 只手臂持各种法器。阁内两侧有壁画十八罗汉及经变故事，为清末作品，神态各异，是阁内艺术珍品。二三层皆面阔三间，进深一大间，阁内藻井、檩枋均绘有旋子彩绘，四周作围廊，依栏鸟瞰，市井民宅历历在目。登上三层，凭窗极目，西部群山隐隐诸峰，尽收眼底。前人赞美大慈阁的诗有"辽海依依见，尧山隐隐横""通衢谁建凌虚阁，留与居人作伟观""燕市珠楼树梢看，祇园金阁碧云端""不染菩提云外出，行慈般若市中悬"等名句。

作为国家级历史文化名城，保定市蕴含着深厚的文化底蕴和光荣的革命传统，早在北宋熙宁四年（1091 年），就在古莲花池内建立了"州学"；元代增建"万卷楼"；明代扩建为"府学"，并增建二程（程颐、程颢）书院：金台书院和上谷书院；清雍正年间，成立莲花池书院。优秀的历史文化，造就了一大批历史名人：春秋战国时燕国大夫郭隗、义士荆轲、汉昭烈帝刘备、宋太祖赵匡胤、科学家祖冲之、郦道元、元代戏曲大家关汉卿、王实甫等都诞生在这块土地上。保定还是中国五四运动时期留法勤工俭学运动发祥地，培养了蔡和森、赵世炎、周恩来、李维汉、李富春、邓小平、陈毅、聂荣臻、蔡畅、向警予等一大批中国早期革命家。我国近代历史上清朝末年第一所陆军军官学校就建在保定东郊，叶挺、赵博生等高级将领及蒋介石、白崇禧、陈诚、顾祝同、刘峙等国民党的将官都曾在该校就读。

保定还曾是义和团活动的重要地区，北方辛亥革命的发祥地，全省第一个共产党支部诞生地。中国共产党领导的风起云涌的反帝、反封建、抗日、解放斗争，都曾在这里留下光辉业绩。《红旗谱》《风云初记》《小兵张嘎》《野火春风斗古城》等记载着保定昨天的辉煌。

河北省最早建立的公共图书馆——直隶图书馆

第14章

正定

——千年古郡沐新风

　　来到正定古城墙脚下，见垣墙苍古威仪，仿佛峨冠博带、岿然于历史烟云中的老者正走笔疾书，书就千年古邑繁盛、寂灭、重生的激越往事。古城墙是正定厚重华彩的一处大手笔，历经兵燹①劫火、岁月侵蚀的倾圮残垣重又雄固，焕发着新的风采。登临城墙，望城楼歇山顶飞檐云举，"三关雄镇"的大字赫然高悬。纵目远眺，揽满城锦绣，一座

正定夜景

---

① 燹（xiǎn）：多指兵乱中纵火焚烧。

古美雄拔的城池尽收眼底：远处，古塔峥嵘、古寺悠然，唐、宋、元、明、清的建筑流风余韵、苍劲恢廓，勾勒出正定旷美天际线；护城河粼粼水波和着车水马龙，"万家灯火管弦清"的市井繁庶亦重现眼前。华灯初上，正定越夜越绚，灯火荡漾中散布的座座古塔通体辉明，似华美琉璃，高崇俊拔于灯海之间：赫赫唐风的须弥塔、富丽精巧的华塔、清透玲珑的澄灵塔、宋代遗风的凌霄塔……璀璨古塔辉映万家灯火，雅俗杂然、古今交融。夜幕下正定的美食街区大红灯笼亮起，人群熙攘的市廛①间飘来阵阵饭菜香，热闹非凡的古城烟火正旺……"登得上城楼，望得见古塔，记得住乡愁"，赏千年古邑，抒怀古豪情。

西望太行山，南临滹沱河，正定优越的地理位置，历来是兵家必争之地和民族交汇融合之所，因为各民族交融杂居，形成了华北大平原上最繁华的大都会。宋代时是契丹、女真、蒙古等少数民族与汉族的杂居地，民族融合，经济文化发展。元代时商品贸易繁荣，吸引了阿拉伯人以及西域等地的商旅。

深厚的文化积淀，浸润了这一方水土，奔流千载的滹沱河，孕育了正定坚毅刚正的人文精神。正定民风自古重信尚义，许多历史人物胸怀爱国仁厚的大德大义，以民族国家利益为重。秦汉时期著名的政治家、军事家赵佗，受命征服岭南，采取"和辑百越"的政策，促进民族团结，也是最早把中原文化和当时的先进生产方式传播到岭南的爱国先驱。三国名将赵子龙，常山真定人，作为古代忠臣良将的楷模，智勇双全的化身，赵云"完人"的形象已深深嵌入人们心中，成为正定人文精神的杰出代表。

源远流长的历史，也为古城正定留下了众多风格迥异的文物古迹和灿烂醇厚的乡土文化遗迹，"三山不见，九桥不流，九楼四塔八大寺，二十四座金牌坊"形容的是正定

---

① 廛（chán）：旧指街市商店的房屋。

丰富的古建遗迹。由于历史的变迁，不少珍贵古迹被毁坏，但还有凌霄塔、华塔、须弥塔、澄灵塔四塔和八大寺中的隆兴寺、广惠寺、临济寺、开元寺、天宁寺尚存，加上寺有寺的传说，塔有塔的故事，历史名人不同凡响的经历和传奇，构成了正定丰富文化的基石。1993 年，正定被国务院批准为国家级历史文化名城。

从古城南门长乐门进入，登临古城墙，可以看到凌霄塔、华塔、须弥塔、澄灵塔四塔对立呼应。

广惠寺华塔，又称花塔，在塔身上半部有各种繁复的花饰，远观如绽放的花束。华塔始建于唐朝，我们现在看到的是金大定年间重修的遗存。这种塔在元朝之后几乎绝迹，国内现存华塔总数也不过十几座，其艺术价值和在中国建筑史上的重要地位被我国著名建筑学家梁思成先生誉为"海内之孤例"。值得一提的是塔身有趣的雕塑，有菩萨、象、虎和力士，惟妙惟肖。

隆兴寺位于正定县城中山东路北侧，占地面积 6 万平方米，是河北省最大的古建筑群之一。寺内有六处文物堪称全国之最：被古建筑大师梁思成先生誉为"世界古建筑的孤例"的造型独特的宋代建筑摩尼殿；被鲁迅先生誉为"东方美神"的五彩悬塑观音；我国早期最大的转轮藏；被推崇为"隋碑第一""楷书之祖"的龙藏寺碑；举高 21.3 米的铜铸千手千眼观音菩萨是我国古代最高的铜铸大佛；设计巧妙，富于变化，做工精细堪称我国一绝的铜铸千佛墩。同时寺内还荟萃了历代碑碣、壁画、瓷器等艺术珍品，均有很高的历史、艺术和科学价值。古建大师梁思成先生曾赞誉："京外名刹当首推正定府隆兴寺。"

临济寺是佛教禅宗五家之一临济宗的祖庭。不幸的是，临济寺的屋舍毁于宋金年间的战火，只有澄灵塔保留了下来。澄灵塔为八角九级密檐式实心砖塔，明显的辽金塔风格，塔高 30.47 米，塔第一层较高，从第二层以上，层高逐减，密檐相接。塔顶木制檐角梁，檐下悬铃。塔顶、檐瓦、脊兽和套兽都是绿琉璃，又被称为"青塔"。临济宗在金代传到日本并对其影响深远，至今仍有许多日本僧人来此参拜。

第15章

山海关
——天下第一关

山海关是国家级历史文化名城，是世界文化遗产、国家首批重点文物保护单位、国家 5A 级旅游景区，是我国境内迄今为止保存最为完整的古代军事防御体系，也是一座天然的长城博物馆。

山海关，古称榆关，位于河北省秦皇岛市东北 15 千米，是明长城的东北关隘之一和中国长城"三大奇观之一"（东有山海关、中有镇北台、西有嘉峪关），有"天下第一关"和"两京锁钥无双地，万里长城第一关"之誉，与万里之外的嘉峪关遥相呼应，闻名天下。它北依燕山，南临渤海，东北和辽宁的绥中接壤，西北和河北抚宁相连。这里地处山海之间，集山、海、关、河、湖等景观于一体，山清水秀，有道是"幽蓟东来第一关，襟连沧海枕青山"。这里所指的"青山"就是明朝早期长城起点翻越的第一座山——角山，角山形势险要，易守难攻，是山海关的天然屏障。而老龙头则是我国唯一一段深入海中的长城，是万里长城中最为独特的防御建筑。山海关城山和海的距离是 8 千米，长城犹如一条巨龙，逶迤于群山之间蜿蜒东来，将高山、雄关、大海连成一体，构成了山海关独特的地理环境。

山海关作为万里长城的东部起点，控遏着辽西走廊。巍巍长城随着山势起伏，雉堞密布，雄压四野。

洪武十四年（1381 年），大将军徐达派遣燕山等卫所屯兵 15 100 人，在永平、界岭等地修筑了三十二关，当年十二月修筑了山海卫城，这就是山海关得名的由来。从此，山海关成为控遏辽东的重要关口。

现在的山海关较完整地保留了明清两代的历史风貌，它的城防建筑布局充分利用了山海关地区的地形特征，是按照"因地形，用险制塞"的方法来设计的。山海关在山和海之间 8 千米的狭长孔道上构筑了由关城、瓮城、罗城、翼城、前哨城堡、海防卫城和长城共同组成的独特的城防布局。既有陆防设施，也有海防设施；既有内外设置，也有防御纵深的立体化防御布局，充分显示了当时人们在山海关设置上的匠心独具。

在总体上，山海关的防御体系可以分为内外两层。内层以关城为核心，辅以瓮城和罗城；外层主要是散点分布的哨城、翼城和各路的关隘、烽堆等，与内层核心形成掎角之势。

山海关关城的东垣为万里长城的一部分，南、北、西三面城垣环依长城。整个关城周长4 796米，城墙高11.6米，厚10米。内为土筑，外包城砖。在北京的东部地区，山海关关城可以说是最大最坚固的。关城四垣中部各有一座城门，东为镇东门、西为迎恩门、南为望洋门、北为威远门。每个城门上均有城楼，东垣上有城楼五座，分别为镇东楼、靖边楼、牧营楼、临闾楼和威远堂，号称"五虎镇东"。城门外为瓮城，在万历十二年（1584年），东门外建了东罗城，崇祯十六年（1643年），西门外建了西罗城，最终形成了今天前拱后卫的防御格局。

外层的防御设施目前遗存下来、保存较为完整的是宁海城和镇虏台，其余的南翼城、北翼城和威远城仅有一些遗迹，主体建筑已经荡然无存。在山海关辖区内，南起渤海之滨的老龙头北至燕山深处的九门口，绵延26千米的长城线上，险要地段设置了南海口关、南水关、山海关、北水关、旱门关、角山关、滥水关、三道关、寺儿峪关和一片石关10个关隘，此外尚有43座敌台、51座城台、14座烽火台，共同铸就了山海关大纵深防御的防御体系，拱卫森严，守望相助，互为掎角，结构严谨，功能明确，攻守自如，可以说是古代军事防御体系中的杰作。

山海关老龙头

山海关作为军事重镇，是重要的交通要道，也是关内通往关外的政治、文化和经济的中转中心。关城作为古城堡群的核心，在内部形成了独特的城市布局。这个具有军事性质的城市，以东西南北十字大街为骨架，街巷、胡同、民居、商铺、神庙、祠坛和相关政府办公地都分布在这座城市里。这里文化发达，商业繁荣，人员往来稠密，处处彰显着活力和生机。它的空间组织结构和立体轮廓的和谐统一，反映了中国古代城市建筑的艺术成就。虽然历经战乱，但是明清时代的格局却相对完整地保留下来，成为人们研究古代城市布局的典范。

　　山海关留给人们的不仅仅是一座经历了无数次硝烟战火洗礼的古代军事要塞，更是一座具有深厚文化底蕴的古城，是文明和进步的见证，是文化史上一座永不磨灭的丰碑。

第16章

邯郸

——一座等了你三千年的城

"邯郸"二字，作为一个城市独属的名称，约有 3 000 年从未改变。

地处河北省南端的古城邯郸，西依太行山脉，东接华北平原，与晋、鲁、豫三省接壤，是国家级历史文化名城、中国成语典故之都。

1965 年，在山西省侯马县（今为侯马市，县级市）出土了大量以璧或璋为材质的春秋末期盟书，盟书上多次出现"邯郸"二字，也就是说，最晚在春秋时期邯郸城的名称就已确定。邯郸二字作为地名，三千年沿袭不变，九州之内独一无二。

邯郸拥有国家级和省级文物保护单位 115 个，文物保护点 1 500 多处，就像珍珠般遍洒在郁郁紫山下，涓涓滏水旁。磁山出土的谷类农作物，惊现了人类农业文明的起源；

邯郸大剧院

赵王城披着厚重的岁月尘埃，成为现存战国时期最完整的王城；端庄巍峨的武灵丛台风采依然；黄粱梦寄寓着对人生的感悟；铜雀台昂扬着曹魏的雄劲；回车巷记载了"将相和"的千古佳话；娲皇宫把神话传说用动静结合的建筑依托在悬崖峭壁上；响堂山石窟把佛教艺术精雕细刻于一洞洞石窟里。走一走石壁陶墙的彭城镇古街，千年不断的磁州窑火熠熠生光；听一听学步桥的故事，既有几分对刻意模仿者的嘲讽，又有几分对亦步亦趋者的调侃；看一看绿草野花中的北朝墓群，《兰陵王入阵曲》回响在耳旁。

早在 8 000 年前，这里就有人类繁衍生息，孕育了新石器早期的磁山文化。磁山文化早于仰韶文化、龙山文化两千多年。据中国社会科学院考古研究所多次考证，磁山文化距今已有 7 300 多年，把中国新石器时代提前了 1 000 多年。战国时期，邯郸作为赵国都城达 158 年之久，是我国北方的政治、经济、文化中心。以胡服骑射为代表的赵文化，其"开拓进取、竞争图强、兼收并蓄"的主流价值观，展现出了赵国在逐鹿中原时的改革创新精神。它是华夏文化与北方草原游牧文化的交汇、融合和升华的结晶，具有中原华夏文化和北方草原文化构成的二重性，集中反映了北方地区诸民族冲突和融合的过程。秦统一中国后，邯郸为 36 郡郡治之一。汉代时，邯郸与长安、洛阳、临淄、成都共享"五都盛名"。东汉末年，曹操在邯郸南部邺城一带建都。北宋时期，邯郸东部的大名府成为北宋都城汴梁的"陪都"。邯郸涉县在抗日战争和解放战争时期，是八路军 129 师司令部和晋冀鲁豫边区政府所在地，"太行号角"踏遍了太行山的沟沟坎坎，新闻火种播撒在华北的山山水水。"人工天河"跃峰渠筑于绝壁之上，在平均海拔 170 米的山间绕岭越峰、涌流奔腾，一渠清波出太行。

磁州窑是中国陶器生产发祥地之一，它的影响遍及晋、冀、鲁、豫、陕以及南方数省。磁州窑历史悠久，"磁山文化"时，这一带的先民已经烧制出精美的陶器。此后"仰韶文化"时期的彩陶，"龙山文化"时期的黑陶，商代的灰陶，乃至发展到北朝和隋代的青瓷、白瓷，实现了由陶向瓷的转变。

邯郸文化是中华民族古老文化的源头之一，是中原文化的重要支柱。它丰厚博沉、璀璨夺目、闻名遐迩、魅力四射，这里是抓一把泥土就能攥出古老文明汁液的地方。

如今的邯郸，变化日新月异。依托太行山深厚的红色资源和丰富的生态资源，邯郸加紧建设以"英雄太行山·中国红河谷"为形象定位的太行红河谷文化旅游经济带，打造国家红色研学旅游示范区、太行绿色产业示范区、特色山水旅游胜地。涉县的旱作梯田由一块块山石修葺而成，规模宏大。从空中看去，沟岭交错，群峰耸峙，梯田随山势绵延，一望无际，像大山掀起了一层层细细的波浪，鳞次栉比，层层叠叠直上山巅，构成了规模宏大又独具特色的梯田景观。

往事并不如烟，都书写在了煌煌史册上；未来征途漫漫，召唤我们去绘就蓝图。邯郸，这座历史文化名城，正以崭新的姿态站在历史新的起点。

蔚县

——河北省的古建筑博物馆

太行山下，一代王城尘封了历史往事，层层瓦当是昔日蔚为壮观的宫殿，残垣断壁是远去辉煌的印记。太行八陉，飞狐峪口，经历过战火，也迎送过商旅。燕云十六州之一的古蔚州，经过 1 000 多年的时光交替，积淀出一个文化多彩的新蔚县。八百庄堡、八百戏楼，留存着沉甸甸的历史；人生故事，剪刻在一纸方寸之间；火树银花，迸发在一瓢铁水当中，多姿多彩的蔚县，展示着传承的经典。

飞狐古道又名飞狐陉，是太行八陉中异常险要的一条通道，它在蔚县逶迤蜿蜒 35 千米。明清时期，中原地区的骡马帮和驼队满载货物行走在飞狐古道上，走出了飞狐商道，也走出了蔚县的一片繁荣。飞狐古道既是商道，又是战道。蔚县就扼守在飞狐古道的咽喉，成为沟通华北平原与塞外大漠的交通要道，蔚县也因为飞狐古道铸就了当时发达的商业集镇。千百年来，蔚县汇聚四海客商，凝聚了多元的文化，留下了众多精美的古建遗产，那些浸透在砖瓦间的历史印记，勾勒出蔚县发展的文化图集。

蔚州古城

在蔚县境内有 2 座古城，代王城和蔚州古城。广袤历史，代蔚长歌，这历史长歌则始于代王城。代王城这座历史名镇距离蔚县县城东 10 千米处，历经 3 000 年左右的时光雕饰，留存到现在的代王城墙呈椭圆形，周长近 10 千米，这在古代城垣中很少见，城垣保存较好，有兴隆门、宝源门等 9 座城门，文化遗存丰富。

蔚州古城距离代王城 10 千米，周长 3 800 多米，距今已有 1 400 多年历史。蔚州古城打破传统礼制比较方正的规制，形制不规则，建筑不对称，城外有护城河，河上有吊桥与内城相连。

悠久的历史，为蔚县留下了大量令人惊叹的人文景观。蔚县县城始建于北周大象二年（580 年）、明洪武十年（1377 年）重修，是京西现有保存最为完整的古城。蔚县现有文物遗存点 1 610 余处，国家级文物保护单位 20 余处，是全国第一国保文物大县。城内的玉皇阁、南安寺塔、释迦寺均为国家级重点文物保护单位，这些带有辽、元、明、清各时期建筑风格，体现儒、释、道不同文化特点的古建筑群，连同县城周边的代王城遗址，罕见的融合三种文化为一体的重泰寺，以及古城堡、古寺庙、古民居、古戏楼星罗棋布，栉风沐雨千百年，构成了蔚县极为丰富的历史文化底蕴，也赢得了"古建筑博物馆"的美誉。

南有福建土楼，北有蔚县古堡。蔚县以古堡为代表的古建筑，不仅具有我国中原地区汉族传统建筑的共性，还具有战略防御的个性，与万里长城共同防御着塞北的敌人。作为蔚县的缩影，暖泉古镇内的庄堡、街巷的格局至今保留完好。亭台楼阁等古老建筑比比皆是，建筑布局严谨，高低大小有序，体现了中国传统文化对建筑的影响和世代相传的古老营建法则。在蔚县，素有八百庄堡、八百戏楼之说，村村皆有老戏楼，戏楼的形式各不相同。

一座座古老建筑，是蔚县的地标，也是沟通古今的桥梁，见证了这片土地从蔚州到蔚县的变化，他们好似一张张历史照片，定格了过往的精彩，留下了昔日的繁华。

第 4 篇
泥土芬芳　非遗之美

　　河北悠久的历史和灿烂的文明孕育了绚丽多彩、形式多样的民间艺术。截至 2021 年 6 月 10 日，河北省有 163 项国家级非物质文化遗产，其中蔚县剪纸、丰宁满族剪纸、唐山皮影戏、杨氏太极拳、武氏太极拳、王其和太极拳 6 个项目入选联合国教科文组织"人类非物质文化遗产代表作名录"。

　　河北民间艺术中的地方戏曲、民间曲艺、特色工艺、乡村古乐、民间美术、沧州武术、吴桥杂技等在国内外享有盛誉。这些艺术从不同角度体现着中华民族文化传统，其共同特色是起源于民间生活，有的是从历史传承下来，有的是从外省移植过来，有的是以新的形式创新的，最终逐步形成浓厚的地方特色，深为广大群众所喜爱。

　　河北民间艺术在历史发展的长河中，对人民群众陶冶情操、娱乐身心、抒发感情、交流思想起到了无形的纽带作用。

第18章

蔚县剪纸

——古老土地上的灵魂之花

蔚县剪纸

蔚县剪纸是河北省具有独特风格的民间艺术，相传已有200余年历史，其制作工艺在全国众多剪纸中独树一帜。作为全国唯一的一种以阴刻为主、阳刻为辅的点彩剪纸，蔚县剪纸重刻更重染。它是以薄薄的宣纸为原料，拿小巧锐利的雕刀刻制，再点染明快绚丽的色彩而成，其基本制作工艺为：设计造型—熏样—雕刻—染色。2006年5月20日，蔚县剪纸经国务院批准列入首批国家级非物质文化遗产名录。

蔚县剪纸以窗花见长。"天皮亮"可以说是最早的窗花形式，即在云母薄片上绘图着色进行装饰。当地早期还盛行供花鞋、荷包、枕头上刺绣用的"花样"。后来河北武强县的木版水印窗花技术传入，蔚县剪纸汲取其色彩特点，仿"天皮亮"透明效果，以刻代剪，形成了蔚县剪纸的独特风格。

蔚县剪纸种类丰富多彩，既有对戏曲人物，鸟虫鱼兽的刻画，也有对农村现实生活的细致描绘。无论是反映人们对吉祥幸福的祈求，还是为了庆祝四时节令、婚寿礼仪；也无论是来源于劳动人民喜闻乐见的历史故事、民间传说，还是对北方特有的文化背景和民俗风情的再现，都体现了民间艺人高超的智慧和丰富的想象力。这些作品构图饱满，造型生动，浑厚中有细腻，纤巧里显纯朴，生活气息浓郁，寓意深刻。加上疏密有致的造型设计，细致入微的精湛刀工，绚丽鲜艳的独特点染，每一件作品都十分生动、耐看，集实用性、观赏性和收藏性于一身。把它贴在纸窗上透过户外光的照射，分外玲珑剔透，五彩缤纷，显得鲜灵活脱，别具一种欢快、明朗、清新的情趣。

在漫长的岁月里蔚县剪纸不仅创造了大量日臻完美的优秀作品，而且培养了许多杰出的民间剪纸艺术家，蔚县南张庄的王老赏（1890—1951）就是其中的杰出代表。他刻画戏曲中的生、旦、净、末、丑等有个性的人物最为拿手，创作出大量深受群众喜爱的作品。在王老赏之前，蔚县剪纸虽已有多年历史，但其刀工粗糙，人物呆板，色彩点染上仅有有限的几种。王老赏在吸收前辈经验的基础上，改革刀具，增加"阴刻"笔法，同时在点染上尝试色彩调配。经他改革后刻出的窗花和各类戏曲人物，一扫过去千篇一律、千人一面、死板呆滞的模样，刀法凝练，造型优美，生动传神，性格鲜明，很受群众欢迎。

北京冬奥会申办成功后，当地剪纸艺人开始制作以冬奥会为主题的剪纸作品。2018年韩国平昌冬奥会闭幕式上，北京八分钟精彩上演，同时播放的专题片中，有一幅蔚县人民专门为冬奥会创作的7米长卷剪纸。冬奥元素为剪纸艺术注入了新的生命，借力冬奥，蔚县剪纸得到进一步宣传，这门非遗艺术也在传承和创新中不断发展。

第19章

衡水内画

——寸天厘地，鬼斧神工

内画艺术是中国特有的一种传统艺术形式。它以玻璃、水晶料器、琥珀等为壶坯，用特制的变形细笔在瓶内反手绘出细致入微的画面，有人物、山水、花鸟、书法等各种题材，格调典雅，笔触精妙，色彩艳丽，可谓"方寸之间，别有天地"。

17世纪，鼻烟流行于欧洲，明末清初传入中国，当时的容器主要是鼻烟盒，随后才有了独具中国风格的鼻烟壶。现在，人们嗜用鼻烟的习惯几近绝迹，但鼻烟壶却作为一种精美、袖珍的艺术品流传下来，关键因素就是内画艺术。鼻烟壶制作包括选料、工艺制作、修饰装潢等一系列过程，其材质涵盖金属、玉、石、陶器、料器、有机物等六大类，工艺内容包括了传统的写、画、雕、刻等多种技术，鼻烟壶成为清代工艺美术的缩影，被后世称为"集中国多种工艺之大成的袖珍艺术品"，饮誉世界。

习三弯勾笔

内画有别于外画，其一，作画顺序相反，内壁要反着书画；其二，绘画角度单一，只能在壶口入笔作画，壶口小限制操作，作画时又不容易看到笔的位置，所以非常考验内画大师的艺术功底。艺术家作画时，要凝神静气，将力道完全集中在手腕之上。最重要的是，落笔无悔，要求一次完成，不然一个小小的瑕疵都可能导致整个作品从头再来。

鼻烟壶内画以中国画为基础，承袭了国画的精髓，中国故事、中国山水、中国人文……在鼻烟壶的方寸之间展现得淋漓尽致。其中被大众熟知的京派鼻烟壶历史最为久远，后期延伸出冀派、鲁派、粤派等各具特色的几大流派。京派大师一般文学艺术修养较高，多以传统题材、历史故事为主，用色古朴，结构严谨，给人以高雅独特的艺术享受；冀派以人物肖像见长，形神兼备，特别是婴戏图和百子图最能反映冀派内画鼻烟壶的艺术特点；鲁派最有特色的是能够利用瓷器上用的釉彩作画，然后，烘烧形成内画鼻烟壶的瓷釉画，即使盛水画面也毫不受损；目前，最年轻的派系当属粤派，以艳丽的色彩和装饰风格著称于世。

衡水是冀派内画的发源地，由于衡水内画艺术独树一帜，被文化部命名为"中国内画艺术之乡"。冀派内画创始人王习三，是京派老艺人叶仲三之子叶晓峰、叶奉祺的第一位外姓弟子。20 世纪 50 年代末，王习三熟练掌握了"叶派"内画技法后，将猫引入鼻烟壶，他采用工笔"撕毛法"画出了水灵灵的猫眼儿和猫毛茸茸的质感，解决了国画写意技法画猫形象呆板、缺乏真实感的难题。王习三自创了冀派内画的特殊工具金属杆勾毛笔，即"习三弯勾笔"，笔杆是直的，笔头是弯的，而且可以随意改变方向。

衡水内画在继承京派厚朴古雅的基础上，糅进鲁派细腻流畅的传统画法，又将国画的绘画技法引入内画，将内画技法发挥得淋漓尽致。后来又将油彩加入内画技法，打破了传统单一的水彩作画的局限，使内画的构图、形象、神韵达到了炉火纯青的地步，被称为"中西合璧"的壮举。2006 年 5 月 20 日，衡水内画荣登首批国家级非物质文化遗产名录。

衡水内画作品

第20章
安国药材
——千年药都的魅力

　　安国市，古名祁州，现为河北省保定市辖区，南距省会石家庄100千米。早在700多年前的北宋时期，这里就成了我国著名的中药材集散地。清朝道光年间达到鼎盛，称祁州为"药都""天下第一药市"，享有"祁州药材名天下"之盛誉。

　　安国药市的兴起，源于药王庙。药王庙坐落于安国市城南（原南关），是全国最大的纪念历代医圣的古建筑群。药王庙始建于东汉，祭拜东汉光武帝刘秀二十八大将之一的邳彤（字伟君）。北宋时药王庙拓址新建，并集会瞻仰纪念。南宋咸淳六年（1270年）

中药药材

又加封为"明灵昭惠显王"。随着帝王对邳彤的不断封赐，"药王"影响越来越大。自从药王庙设祀以来，民众有病纷纷求助药王，善男信女，常来进香，香火甚盛，药商乘机售药，以至逐渐形成了药材庙会。清代中期逐渐形成全国各地药商组成的"十三帮"及"五大会"，同时建立了招待商客、管理市场的"安客堂"，安国自此成为我国北方最大的药材交流中心和药材集散地。自明清至民国，庙会由"十三帮"轮流操办。每逢庙会，整个县城药气熏天，热闹非常，"药都"的称号就此名扬中外。

安国药王庙会及药市历史悠久，影响广泛，在中医药发展史上占有重要地位。药王庙会作为社会运行机制中的经济载体、文化载体，承纳了浩瀚如烟的民间文化，凝聚了当地人民和广大药商的思想感情、理想愿望、道德风尚和审美趣味。它不仅是安国药业的发源地，也直接孕育了一个全国最大的药材集散地——安国药市，在促进全国医药交流，弘扬中华医药文化方面发挥了重要作用。2006 年 5 月 20 日，安国药市经国务院批准列入首批国家级非物质文化遗产名录。

除了药市，安国的中药文化产业还有"药博园"。安国药博园兴建于 2016 年，现有药材种植景观区 800 亩，中药材品种 300 类，道地药材及八大祁药种植示范区 1 000 亩，200 亩智能温室大棚、薰衣草庄园、油菜花田园等，是"安国数字中药都"项目建设的重要保障。

创会于 2005 年的中国中医药博览会，是中医药行业水平最高的重点国家级展会，以中药制药及中医药大健康产品、中药材（饮片）、中医药制药装备、中医药国际服务贸易等为主题，通过展览、交易与论坛相结合的方式，共享丰富的宣传资源、推广渠道，全力打造中医药创新成果展示和项目洽谈对接的高端平台。

2022 年，中国中医药博览会决定将中国中医药博览会永久会址落户河北省安国市。

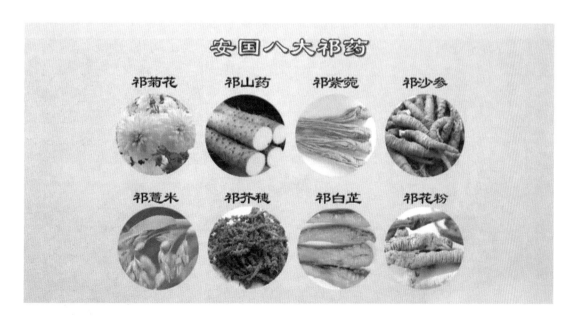

第21章

皮影
——灯影下的百态人生

　　皮影，又称"影子戏"或"灯影戏"，是一种以兽皮或纸板做成的人物剪影，在灯光照射下用隔亮布进行表演，是我国民间广为流传的傀儡戏之一。表演时，艺人们在白色幕布后面，一边操纵戏曲人物，一边用当地流行的曲调唱述故事，同时配以打击乐器和弦乐，有浓厚的乡土气息。在过去电影、电视等媒体尚未发达的年代，皮影戏曾是十分受欢迎的民间娱乐活动之一。皮影戏流派众多，河北是皮影大省，目前河北已有唐山皮影、冀南皮影和河间皮影入选国家级非物质文化遗产名录。

唐山皮影
　　唐山皮影又称滦州影、乐亭影、驴皮影，是中国皮影戏中影响最大的种类之一。通常认为滦州影戏初创于明代末期，盛行于清末民国初年，迄今已有400多年的历史。因其影人、道具是用驴皮镂刻并着色制成，故又通称"驴皮影"。它流行于河北的唐山、承德、

皮影制作过程之影人上色

廊坊等地区以及东北三省各市县，有着深厚的群众基础，是当地群众喜闻乐见的一种艺术表演形式。唐山皮影是历史悠久、影响深远的皮影流派，河北、北京、东北、山东一带的各路皮影唱腔，均源于唐山皮影。1966 年，乐亭县被文化部（今文化与旅游部）命名为"中国民间艺术之乡——皮影之乡"。

唐山皮影戏以历史故事、神话传说、寓言故事为主，题材大多来源于历史名著，主题积极向上，有的表现保家卫国的英雄，有的表现惩恶扬善的侠士，有的表现反抗压迫的勇者，歌颂真善美，鞭挞假恶丑。

剧目内容是深层剖析当地社会民俗民风、宗教心理的重要材料。历代唐山皮影艺人对唱腔表演、舞台道具的材料和技艺的改良与创新从未间断过，这些经验是今人和后人的宝贵财富。唐山皮影的传承延续着口传心授的方式，为文化传承的方式方法提供了重要的借鉴价值。唐山皮影的唱腔、音乐、表演、造型有着本地域特有的风格，受到国内外同行和观众的赞誉，具有很高的欣赏与研究价值。

冀南皮影

冀南皮影戏主要流行于河北南部，特别是以邯郸市肥乡区为中心的地区，并影响到冀中、冀北等地。肥乡区是冀南皮影的发祥地，肥乡当地将皮影称为"牛皮影""皮子戏""戳皮戏""一只眼戏"。肥乡皮影造型以中国传统戏剧为依托，以民间剪纸的样式出现，是典型的冀南皮影代表。

冀南皮影戏的影人造型粗犷古朴，采用牛皮刻制，其雕镂并不精细，许多地方不用刀刻，而直接用彩绘，这种雕、绘相法的风貌是冀南皮影的特色之一。影人的高度在一尺左右，造型分为生（老生、小生）、旦、净（即花脸）、丑等行当。其中文人造型大多只有一只胳膊，武将则有两只胳膊。骑马的影人，上半身是活动的，下半身则是与马刻绘在一起的一个整体。民间艺人对影人的造型、色彩和雕刻的处理，除在人物需要的特点基础上进行概括夸张外，又受到民间剪纸和戏剧脸谱的影响，同时也逐渐形成了既有程式化又各具角色特征的造型体制。冀南皮影演唱没有文本，完全是口传心授，对白口语化，通俗易懂，有鲜明的地方特色。

冀南皮影较多地保持着中国皮影戏的早期面貌，它对比唐山皮影，在造型、剧本、唱腔、演出形式等方面有着非常强烈的差异，具有较高的学术价值和文化内涵。

河间皮影

河间皮影戏是冀中皮影戏的重要代表，冀中皮影戏是我国西部皮影戏在华北平原的流传，相传是明代时由甘肃、陕西迁民带过来的，民间艺人称之为"兰州影"，主要流布于河北的保定、沧州、廊坊、石家庄一带。目前，冀中皮影戏在保定、廊坊等地基本消失，而在河间还有着比较完整的保存。

河间皮影的影人雕工精巧，造型隽秀、逼真，既是皮影戏演出时的道具，又是富有浓郁地方特色的民间工艺品。皮影班社保持着传统的演出习俗，每到秋天，以唱皮影戏来祈福、酬神，并作为乡民的娱乐形式。

第 22 章

沧州武术
——武健泱泱乎有表海雄风

　　"武术之乡"沧州几千年来，可谓英雄辈出，精英荟萃，历史悠久。据统计，沧州在明清时期出过武进士、武举人 1 937 名。源起和流传于沧州的武术门类、拳械达 52 种之多，占全国 129 种门类、拳械的 40%，乃中国武术发源地之一。1992 年，沧州市被国家体委首批命名为"武术之乡"，成为全国第一个获此殊荣的地级市。

　　沧州武术有其本身的特色，既有大开大合勇猛绝伦的长势，又有推手擒拿小巧灵活的招数，并具有速度快、力度大和善于攻守的实战特点。武术门类基本可分少林、武当两大派系。少林拳中有八极、太祖、六合等，武当拳中有太极、八卦、形意等。

太极拳

近年来，在国家"发掘、研究、整理、继承"武术政策的指引下，沧州武林勃发了新的生机。现在，沧州市各级武术协会均已建立，业余武术活动点恢复和建立达百来个，有几万人参加武术活动。不少老拳师积极响应国家的号召，在授徒传艺的同时，抓紧著书立说。

　　创办于 1989 年的"沧州武术节"，是全国举办最早的武术节，也是比赛、表演项目最多的一个群众性武术节日，在海内外有较高的知名度。"沧州武术节"融武术、文化、经济为一体，重点突出沧州传统武术的特点与优势，充分体现武术节的群众性、传统性、学术性与国际性。历届武术节邀请俄罗斯、美国、比利时、日本、新加坡等国家和地区的武术界朋友，参加"传统武术国际恳谈会""国际精武联谊研讨会"、武术竞技赛、表演赛等各种活动，提出弘扬"爱国、修身、正义、助人"的精武精神，发扬"精武一家"的优良传统，扩大了沧州"武术之乡"的影响。

吴桥杂技

——没有吴桥不成班

　　吴桥县位于河北省东南部，杂技文化底蕴深厚，是我国杂技发祥地之一。中国被视为"杂技王国"，中国杂技被称为"东方艺术的明珠"，很大程度上就是因为这个小县所传承的杂技与这里的杂技所创造的辉煌。2006年5月20日，吴桥杂技经国务院批准列入首批国家级非物质文化遗产名录。

　　在吴桥，杂技艺术俗称"耍玩艺儿"。民谣说："上至九十九，下到才会走，吴桥耍玩艺儿，人人有一手。"吴桥人对杂技有着特殊的爱好，无论在街头巷尾，还是田间麦场，

吴桥杂技——转碟

甚至在饭桌前和土炕上，他们随时都会翻一串跟斗，叠几组罗汉，打几趟拳脚，变几套戏法魔术。

"没有吴桥不成班"是杂技界广泛流传的一句话，意思是没有吴桥杂技艺人就组不成杂技班。这句话有两层含义：一是吴桥杂技从业者人员众多，自然各班子里都有吴桥人；二是吴桥艺人的技艺好，没有吴桥人难撑起一个班子。吴桥不仅有很悠久的杂技历史，还有很多的杂技文化遗存，这里还曾涌现了很多在中国近现代史上著名的杂技名人名班。这些名人名班的出现，表明了吴桥对中国杂技的巨大贡献。吴桥是中华杂技艺术家的摇篮。吴桥人以一代又一代人的心血，用毕生的精力倾注于杂技事业，以非凡的毅力和对杂技事业的执着投入，促使杂技艺术在历史的长河中不断发展。

国家实行改革开放后，给予吴桥杂技以高度重视和支持。激发了吴桥人民弘扬杂技文化，发展吴桥经济的热情，吴桥杂技从此进入一个快速发展的繁荣阶段。

1993 年 11 月"吴桥杂技大世界"建成并对外开放。大世界南部是江湖文化城、吕祖庙、孙公祠、泰山行宫等仿古建筑群；北部由杂技奇观宫、魔术迷幻宫等现代建筑群环抱气魄宏伟的中心广场。南北之间由 16 根巍然屹立的大理石杂技历史图腾柱连接，高空鸟瞰全貌是一辆杂技独轮车的造型，不仅反映了吴桥杂技的发展历史，而且超凡脱俗，气势恢宏。2004 年，吴桥被国家挂牌命名为首批"中国杂技之乡"。

第24章

曲阳石雕

——一锤千年尽显绝代风华

　　曲阳是中国石雕艺术之乡，其白石雕刻尤为著名。从西汉开始，曲阳人开采当地白石，走上雕刻之路，世间所称汉白玉即源于此。据考证，满城西汉中山靖王刘胜墓出土的汉白玉男女石俑就是由曲阳黄山汉白玉雕刻而成，是迄今为止发现年代最为久远的曲阳石雕作品。曲阳王台北村的狗塔，相传是东汉光武帝刘秀为一条义犬而修建的。狗塔共13层，高约50米，由黄山汉白玉和砖瓦精筑而成。塔内一至四层的石壁上刻有浮雕壁画，构图严谨，布局匀称，艺术性较高，代表着当时曲阳石雕艺人的艺术水平。曲阳"狗塔"是中国最早的纪念碑式大型石雕建筑物之一，也是东汉时期石雕艺术成就较高的建筑物。

　　魏晋南北朝时期，佛教盛行，全国各地建寺修庙、凿山开窟，规模浩大，盛况空前，曲阳石雕由此得到了飞速发展，这一时期，曲阳石雕艺人们的足迹遍布全国各地，他们充分发挥自己的雕刻才艺，雕刻出众多的佛教造像。

　　隋唐时期，曲阳石雕趋于纯熟自然，人物形象或挺拔刚健，或婀娜多姿，雍容华贵，别开生面。五代王处直墓出土的伎乐图女伶丰腴饱满，浮雕门神威武雄壮，气韵逼人，不逊盛唐，世所仅见。在这一时期，曲阳石雕进入快速发展时期，曲阳由此成为我国北方的雕刻中心。

　　元代，代表曲阳石雕最高水平的杨琼主持了元大都建设，石雕艺术在建筑领域大放异彩，开辟了一个新的方向，影响及于以后各代。

　　明、清时期，在皇家宫殿、陵墓和园林的营建中，曲阳石雕艺人们将他们精湛的雕刻技艺尽情发挥，几乎达到登峰造极之境。在颐和园苏州街北岸的两块护岸石上留有"曲阳匠师"的刻字，成为曲阳石匠参与京城园林建设的珍贵史料。

　　新中国成立初期，曲阳十几名雕刻艺人被选调到北京，经过一年多的培训后，他们负责人民英雄纪念碑浮雕的主雕任务。纪念碑完工之后，北京市政府遵照周恩来总理的指示，以参加纪念碑建设工程的曲阳雕刻艺人为骨干力量成立了北京市建筑艺术雕刻厂，这为曲阳雕刻艺人们提供了更为广阔的用武之地。

　　曲阳石雕在塑造佛像这类性别不清的形象时，强调人物内心世界的刻画，讲究人物间、人物和动物之间的呼应。造型侧重神韵，不追求形似，去掉了繁琐细节，抓住了人的精神及结构的主旨，使用减法，在雕像造型动态结构上达到传神的境界。石雕作品造型千姿百态、构图形象各异，由于用原始手段开采石料，无法控制石料体积的厚、薄、方圆，曲阳石雕艺人适形造型，根据这些异型的石料，展开丰富的想象，雕刻出各式各样的石雕作品。

在曲阳石雕中，圆雕、浮雕、线刻等表现方法常常被不拘一法地混合并用于一件大型石雕，局部往往有着浮雕、线刻的部分。石雕作品中那些人像的头、手等部位为圆雕，而大部分身躯则是用依附于石壁的高浮雕形式，衣饰等细部又是由线刻形式表现出来。镶嵌、镂空等方法有时也被结合进来。

曲阳石雕的文化内涵是深沉的。它凝聚着一个古老而又淳朴的、在太行山脉以农业为主要生存手段的历代农民艺匠的雕刻之魂。他们广泛汲取北方诸民族与佛教文化的营养，并且在作品中融入了强烈的本民族文化精神。这些作品渗透着曲阳雕刻艺匠对于当地生活的深切体验，出于他们对石刻造型艺术独特的感悟，同时也把他们的民族自豪感、宗教信念、审美情趣熔铸于每尊雕像之中。纵观历史，各个时期的曲阳石雕艺术作品展现出曲阳艺匠拙中藏巧、以小喻大、顽石通灵的高超技艺，蕴含着曲阳文化的深沉内涵，也决定了曲阳石雕的传承价值。在这块盛产白石的山坳中，曲阳人通过一锤一钎的不断雕凿，出色地雕刻出众多世界级的文化瑰宝，使得曲阳石雕以其特有的魅力和活力延续了两千余年而长盛不衰。

河北省博物馆——曲阳石雕展厅

第25章
井陉拉花
——舞姿健美，舒展有方

　　井陉拉花是石家庄市井陉县特有的一种民间艺术形式，广泛流传于井陉周边乡村，自古以来就以其深沉朴实的风韵、刚健苍凉的艺术特色以及富有表现力的艺术舞姿深受百姓的喜爱，可谓是"上至九十九，下至刚会走，人人都会扭"。2006年5月20日，井陉拉花经国务院批准列入首批国家级非物质文化遗产名录。

井陉拉花表演

井陉拉花最早源于民间的节日、庙会、奠基拜神时的街头广场花会，历史悠久，源远流长。拉花产生并形成于何时何地已无历史记载、无文字可考。到了 20 世纪初，拉花已经十分盛行，成为当地百姓喜闻乐见的一种舞蹈形式，有"山西梆子不离口，井陉拉花遍地扭"的说法。1996 年，中华人民共和国文化部将井陉县命名为"中国民间艺术之乡——拉花之乡"。

　　这种舞蹈诞生于"开门见山、走路爬坡"的自然环境里，因此其舞蹈动作模仿出井陉山区山高路陡难行走的特点，表现出在坑坑洼洼、曲曲弯弯的山路上，高抬腿、前走后退、前俯后仰、左晃右摆、时上时下、拐弯抹角、相互搀扶、迎难而进的情景。

　　其音乐也是独立乐种。既有河北吹歌的韵味，又有民歌、民间曲牌和戏曲曲牌的音调，还不乏浓厚的寺庙音乐和宫廷音乐的色彩，它的曲牌约有十几首，如"万年欢""春夏秋冬""爬山虎"等曲牌。它古朴典雅、清爽动听、深沉美妙、刚健稳重，其风格特征是刚而不野、柔而不靡、华而不浮、悲而不泣，突出特点是节奏鲜明。与拉花舞蹈的沉稳、含蓄、刚健、豪迈风格交相辉映，乐舞融合，浑然一体。

　　井陉拉花有显著的艺术特色，以"拧肩""翻腕""扭臂""吸腿""撇脚"等为主要舞蹈动作，以"花瓶""花伞""彩扇""霸王鞭"等为主要表演道具，加之可称为独立乐种的拉花音乐伴奏，形成刚柔并济、粗犷含蓄的独特艺术特色，擅长于表现悲壮、凄婉、眷恋、欢悦等情绪。

　　井陉拉花是一种不受场地限制，既可街头、场院演出，也可登台献技，时间可长可短的群舞。演出方式可分为两种：一种是行进中的演出，称为"过街"，这种表演因受行进的局限，无法追求舞蹈的完整性，有因地制宜的特点；另一种为场地演出，其队形多变，能充分发挥演员的表演技能，而且演出完整。参加演出的演员，一般为六的倍数，大规模的拉花队伍如 18 人拉花、36 人拉花、60 人拉花和 102 人拉花等都是继承了拉花的这一特点。

 第26章

河北梆子

——燕赵大地的宫商正韵

河北梆子是河北省的主要地方剧种，也是中国梆子声腔的一个重要支脉，形成于清代道光年间，是"山陕梆子"传入河北之后，经河北人民培育而形成的。河北梆子流行于河北、天津、北京以及山东、河南、山西部分地区，成为中国北方影响较大的传统戏曲剧种之一。2006年5月20日，河北梆子经国务院批准列入首批国家级非物质文化遗产名录。

河北梆子不仅擅长表现历史题材，且能很好地反映现实生活。目前留存的传统剧有500多个，有的揭露封建统治阶级的腐朽和丑恶，有的反映阶级压迫，有的歌颂抗击侵略者的英雄人物，有的赞美妇女对婚姻自由的追求与向往，有的反映农村生活的风趣。

现代河北梆子《人民英雄纪念碑》

其传统剧目多取材于历史故事，代表性剧目有《蝴蝶杯》《秦香莲》《辕门斩子》《杜十娘》等。

　　2018 年，北京市河北梆子剧团打造推出原创大型河北梆子现代戏《人民英雄纪念碑》，为新中国成立 70 周年华诞献礼。该剧是一部"讴歌党、讴歌祖国、讴歌人民、讴歌英雄"的作品，首次对"人民英雄纪念碑"这一中华民族的精神象征进行具象化的艺术解读，寄托了新时代文艺工作者慎终追远、不忘初心、致敬人民、致敬英雄，让人民英雄的灵魂有所安放的创作情怀。

　　《人民英雄纪念碑》讲述了在 1952 年春，军代表玉琴回到了老家河北曲阳大石村，招募石匠雕刻人民英雄纪念碑。在玉琴的努力下，雕刻绝技不可或缺的石老爹抛却了所有的个人恩怨，投身到人民英雄纪念碑的雕刻中的故事。

Appendices
附 录

小五台山云海

附录 1
河北省行政区划名录

地级市	市辖区	县级市	县	自治县
石家庄市	长安区、桥西区、新华区、裕华区、栾城区、藁城区、鹿泉区、井陉矿区	晋州市、新乐市、辛集市	赵县、平山县、正定县、灵寿县、高邑县、赞皇县、深泽县、无极县、行唐县、元氏县、井陉县	
唐山市	路北区、路南区、古冶区、开平区、丰南区、丰润区、曹妃甸区	遵化市、滦州市、迁安市	玉田县、乐亭县、迁西县、滦南县	
秦皇岛市	海港区、北戴河区、抚宁区、山海关区		昌黎县、卢龙县	青龙满族自治县
邯郸市	丛台区、复兴区、邯山区、永年区、肥乡区、峰峰矿区	武安市	邱县、磁县、魏县、涉县、曲周县、馆陶县、成安县、大名县、鸡泽县、广平县、临漳县	
邢台市	襄都区、信都区、任泽区、南和区	南宫市、沙河市	威县、清河县、柏乡县、宁晋县、隆尧县、临城县、广宗县、临西县、内丘县、平乡县、巨鹿县、新河县	

（续表）

地级市	市辖区	县级市	县	自治县
保定市	竞秀区、莲池区、清苑区、徐水区、满城区	安国市、涿州市、定州市、高碑店市	雄县、蠡县、安新县、容城县、易县、涞水县、阜平县、唐县、定兴县、高阳县、涞源县、望都县、曲阳县、顺平县、博野县	
张家口市	桥西区、桥东区、宣化区、崇礼区、万全区、下花园区		蔚县、康保县、张北县、阳原县、赤城县、怀来县、涿鹿县、沽源县、怀安县、尚义县	
承德市	双桥区、双滦区、鹰手营子矿区	平泉市	承德县、兴隆县、隆化县、滦平县	丰宁满族自治县、宽城满族自治县、围场满族蒙古族自治县
沧州市	运河区、新华区	河间市、泊头市、黄骅市、任丘市	沧县、青县、献县、东光县、海兴县、盐山县、肃宁县、南皮县、吴桥县	孟村回族自治县
廊坊市	广阳区、安次区	霸州市、三河市	固安县、永清县、大城县、文安县、香河县	大厂回族自治县
衡水市	桃城区、冀州区	深州市	景县、饶阳县、枣强县、故城县、阜城县、安平县、武邑县、武强县	

河北省森林公园、地质公园和风景名胜区名录

1. 河北省部分国家级森林公园

序号	名称	所在地／隶属	森林公园等级
1	河北茅荆坝国家森林公园	河北省承德市隆化县	国家级
2	保定白石山景区	河北省保定市涞源县白石山镇丰凉沟村	国家级
3	河北塞罕坝国家森林公园	河北省承德市围场满族蒙古族自治县	国家级
4	五岳寨景区	河北省石家庄市灵寿县南营乡草房村	国家级
5	河北天生桥·瀑布群	河北省保定市阜平县	国家级
6	河北仙台山国家森林公园	河北省石家庄市井陉县	国家级
7	河北驼梁山国家森林公园	河北省石家庄市平山县	国家级
8	河北馨锤峰国家森林公园	河北省承德市承德县	国家级
9	河北六里坪国家森林公园	河北省承德市兴隆县	国家级
10	河北海滨国家森林公园	河北省秦皇岛市北戴河区	国家级
11	河北木兰围场国家森林公园	河北省承德市围场满族蒙古族自治县哈里哈乡	国家级
12	河北黑龙山国家森林公园	河北省张家口市赤城县	国家级
13	河北响堂山国家森林公园	河北邯郸市峰峰矿区	国家级
14	河北古北岳国家森林公园	河北省保定市唐县	国家级
15	河北蝎子沟国家森林公园	河北省邢台市临城县	国家级
16	河北大青山国家森林公司	河北省张家口市尚义县	国家级

（续表）

序号	名称	所在地／隶属	森林公园等级
17	河北野三坡国家森林公园	河北省保定市涞水县	国家级
18	河北辽河源国家森林公园	河北省承德市平泉县	国家级
19	河北武安国家森林公园	河北省邯郸市武安市	国家级
20	河北山海关国家森林公园	河北省秦皇岛市山海关区	国家级
21	河北易州国家森林公园	河北省保定市易县	国家级
22	河北翔云岛国家森林公园河	河北省唐山市乐亭县	国家级
23	河北丰宁国家森林公园	河北省承德市丰宁县	国家级
24	河北黄羊山国家森林公园	河北省张家口涿鹿县	国家级
25	河北清东陵国家森林公园	河北省唐山市遵化县	国家级
26	河北白草洼国家森林公园	河北省承德市滦平县	国家级
27	河北前南峪国家森林公园	河北省邢台市襄都区	国家级

2. 河北省部分国家级地质公园

序号	名称	所在地／隶属	地质公园等级
1	涞水野三坡国家地质公园	保定市	世界级、国家级
2	涞源白石山国家地质公园	保定市	国家级
3	邢台峡谷群国家地质公园	邢台市	国家级
4	阜平天生桥国家地质公园	保定市	国家级
5	兴隆国家地质公园	承德市	国家级
6	秦皇岛柳江国家地质公园	秦皇岛市	国家级
7	承德丹霞地貌国家地质公园	承德市	国家级
8	武安国家地质公园	邯郸市	国家级
9	河北迁安－迁西国家地质公园	唐山市	国家级
10	赞皇嶂石岩国家地质公园	石家庄市	国家级
11	临城国家地质公园	邢台市	国家级

3. 河北省国家级风景名胜区（截至 2018 年 5 月）

序号	名称	所在地/隶属	风景名胜区等级
1	承德避暑山庄—外八庙	承德市	世界级、国家级
2	秦皇岛—北戴河风景名胜区	秦皇岛市	国家级
3	野三坡	保定市	国家级
4	苍岩山	石家庄市	国家级
5	嶂石岩	石家庄市	国家级
6	西柏坡—天桂山	石家庄市	国家级
7	崆山白云洞	邢台市	国家级
8	太行大峡谷	邢台市	国家级
9	响堂山	邯郸市	国家级
10	娲皇宫	邯郸市	国家级

附录3
河北省国家级非物质文化遗产名录

序号	名称	属地	批次
1	河北梆子	省直	2006年5月 第一批
2	耿村民间故事	石家庄市	2006年5月 第一批
3	井陉拉花	石家庄市	2006年5月 第一批
4	石家庄丝弦	石家庄市	2006年5月 第一批
5	磁州窑烧制技艺	邯郸市	2006年5月 第一批
6	冀南皮影戏	邯郸市	2006年5月 第一批
7	女娲祭典	邯郸市	2006年5月 第一批
8	武安傩戏	邯郸市	2006年5月 第一批
9	武安平调落子	邯郸市	2006年5月 第一批
10	永年鼓吹乐	邯郸市	2006年5月 第一批
11	杨氏太极拳	邯郸市	2006年5月 第一批
12	隆尧秧歌戏	邢台市	2006年5月 第一批
13	沙河藤牌阵	邢台市	2006年5月 第一批
14	邢台梅花拳	邢台市	2006年5月 第一批
15	冀中笙管乐（霸州高桥音乐会）	廊坊市	2006年5月 第一批
16	冀中笙管乐（霸州胜芳音乐会）	廊坊市	2006年5月 第一批
17	冀中笙管乐（屈家营音乐会）	廊坊市	2006年5月 第一批
18	安国药市	保定市	2006年5月 第一批

序号	名称	属地	批次
19	定州秧歌戏	保定市	2006 年 5 月　第一批
20	冀中笙管乐（涞水高洛音乐会）	保定市	2006 年 5 月　第一批
21	清苑哈哈腔	保定市	2006 年 5 月　第一批
22	曲阳石雕	保定市	2006 年 5 月　第一批
23	徐水狮舞	保定市	2006 年 5 月　第一批
24	沧州武术	沧州市	2006 年 5 月　第一批
25	河间歌诗	沧州市	2006 年 5 月　第一批
26	木板大鼓	沧州市	2006 年 5 月　第一批
27	青县哈哈腔	沧州市	2006 年 5 月　第一批
28	吴桥杂技	沧州市	2006 年 5 月　第一批
29	西河大鼓	沧州市	2006 年 5 月　第一批
30	乐亭大鼓	唐山市	2006 年 5 月　第一批
31	评剧	唐山市	2006 年 5 月　第一批
32	唐山皮影戏	唐山市	2006 年 5 月　第一批
33	衡水内画	衡水市	2006 年 5 月　第一批
34	武强木板年画	衡水市	2006 年 5 月　第一批
35	昌黎地秧歌	秦皇岛市	2006 年 5 月　第一批
36	抚宁鼓吹乐	秦皇岛市	2006 年 5 月　第一批
37	康保二人台	张家口市	2006 年 5 月　第一批
38	蔚县剪纸	张家口市	2006 年 5 月　第一批
39	丰宁满族剪纸	承德市	2006 年 5 月　第一批
40	常山战鼓	石家庄市	2008 年 6 月　第二批
41	坠子戏（深泽）	石家庄市	2008 年 6 月　第二批
42	中幡（正定高照）	石家庄市	2008 年 6 月　第二批
43	焰火炮竹制作技艺（南张井老虎火）	石家庄市	2008 年 6 月　第二批
44	民间社火（桃林坪花脸社火）	石家庄市	2008 年 6 月　第二批
45	龙舞（曲周龙灯）	邯郸市	2008 年 6 月　第二批

（续表）

序号	名称	属地	批次
46	豫剧	邯郸市	2008 年 6 月　第二批
47	冀南四股弦（馆陶县）	邯郸市	2008 年 6 月　第二批
48	冀南四股弦（魏县）	邯郸市	2008 年 6 月　第二批
49	冀南四股弦（肥乡县）	邯郸市	2008 年 6 月　第二批
50	邯郸赛戏（邯郸市）	邯郸市	2008 年 6 月　第二批
51	邯郸赛戏（武安市）	邯郸市	2008 年 6 月　第二批
52	邯郸赛戏（涉县）	邯郸市	2008 年 6 月　第二批
53	永年西调	邯郸市	2008 年 6 月　第二批
54	山东大鼓（鸡泽梨花大鼓）	邯郸市	2008 年 6 月　第二批
55	太极拳（武氏太极拳）	邯郸市	2008 年 6 月　第二批
56	草编（大名草编）	邯郸市	2008 年 6 月　第二批
57	彩布拧台	邯郸市	2008 年 6 月　第二批
58	传统棉纺织技艺（魏县）	邯郸市	2008 年 6 月　第二批
59	传统棉纺织技艺（肥乡）	邯郸市	2008 年 6 月　第二批
60	民间社火（永年抬花桌）	邯郸市	2008 年 6 月　第二批
61	灯会（苇子灯阵）	邯郸市	2008 年 6 月　第二批
62	道教音乐（广宗太平道乐）	邢台市	2008 年 6 月　第二批
63	鼓舞（隆尧招子鼓）	邢台市	2008 年 6 月　第二批
64	乱弹（威县乱弹）	邢台市	2008 年 6 月　第二批
65	冀南四股弦（巨鹿县）	邢台市	2008 年 6 月　第二批
66	山东大鼓（威县梨花大鼓）	邢台市	2008 年 6 月　第二批
67	柳编（广宗柳编）	邢台市	2008 年 6 月　第二批
68	内丘纸马	邢台市	2008 年 6 月　第二批
69	抬阁（隆尧县泽畔抬阁）	邢台市	2008 年 6 月　第二批
70	冀中笙管乐（小冯村音乐会）	廊坊市	2008 年 6 月　第二批
71	冀中笙管乐（张庄音乐会）	廊坊市	2008 年 6 月　第二批
72	冀中笙管乐（军卢村音乐会）	廊坊市	2008 年 6 月　第二批

（续表）

序号	名称	属地	批次
73	冀中笙管乐（东张务音乐会）	廊坊市	2008 年 6 月 第二批
74	冀中笙管乐（南响口梵呗音乐会）	廊坊市	2008 年 6 月 第二批
75	冀中笙管乐（里东庄音乐老会）	廊坊市	2008 年 6 月 第二批
76	京东大鼓	廊坊市	2008 年 6 月 第二批
77	西河大鼓	廊坊市	2008 年 6 月 第二批
78	八卦掌	廊坊市	2008 年 6 月 第二批
79	中幡（安头屯中幡）	廊坊市	2008 年 6 月 第二批
80	左各庄杆会	廊坊市	2008 年 6 月 第二批
81	苏桥飞叉会	廊坊市	2008 年 6 月 第二批
82	秸秆扎刻	廊坊市	2008 年 6 月 第二批
83	花丝镶嵌制作技艺	廊坊市	2008 年 6 月 第二批
84	灯会（胜芳灯会）	廊坊市	2008 年 6 月 第二批
85	抬阁（葛渔城重阁会）	廊坊市	2008 年 6 月 第二批
86	冀中笙管乐（雄县古乐）	保定市	2008 年 6 月 第二批
87	冀中笙管乐（安新县团头村音乐会）	保定市	2008 年 6 月 第二批
88	冀中笙管乐（易县东昧拾幡古乐）	保定市	2008 年 6 月 第二批
89	唢呐艺术（子位吹歌）	保定市	2008 年 6 月 第二批
90	龙舞（易县摆字龙灯）	保定市	2008 年 6 月 第二批
91	保定老调	保定市	2008 年 6 月 第二批
92	鹰爪翻子拳	保定市	2008 年 6 月 第二批
93	定瓷传统烧制技艺	保定市	2008 年 6 月 第二批
94	易水砚制作技艺	保定市	2008 年 6 月 第二批
95	冀中笙管乐（辛安庄民间音乐会）	沧州市	2008 年 6 月 第二批
96	鼓舞（沧州落子）	沧州市	2008 年 6 月 第二批
97	麒麟舞（黄骅）	沧州市	2008 年 6 月 第二批
98	狮舞（沧县狮舞）	沧州市	2008 年 6 月 第二批
99	皮影戏（河间皮影戏）	沧州市	2008 年 6 月 第二批

（续表）

序号	名称	属地	批次
100	八极拳（孟村八极拳）	沧州市	2008 年 6 月　第二批
101	劈挂拳	沧州市	2008 年 6 月　第二批
102	燕青拳	沧州市	2008 年 6 月　第二批
103	生铁冶铸技艺（干模铸造技艺）	沧州市	2008 年 6 月　第二批
104	千童信子节	沧州市	2008 年 6 月　第二批
105	唢呐艺术（唐山花吹）	唐山市	2008 年 6 月　第二批
106	泥塑（玉田泥塑）	唐山市	2008 年 6 月　第二批
107	形意拳（深州）	衡水市	2008 年 6 月　第二批
108	蒸馏酒酿制技艺（衡水老白干）	衡水市	2008 年 6 月　第二批
109	孟姜女故事传说	秦皇岛市	2008 年 6 月　第二批
110	昌黎民歌	秦皇岛市	2008 年 6 月　第二批
111	晋剧	张家口市	2008 年 6 月　第二批
112	秧歌（蔚县秧歌）	张家口市	2008 年 6 月　第二批
113	灯会（蔚县拜灯山）	张家口市	2008 年 6 月　第二批
114	唢呐艺术（丰宁满族吵子会）	承德市	2008 年 6 月　第二批
115	隆化满族二贵摔跤	承德市	2008 年 6 月　第二批
116	山庄老酒酿造技艺	承德市	2008 年 6 月　第二批
117	板城烧锅酒酿造技艺	承德市	2008 年 6 月　第二批
118	抬阁（宽城背杆）	承德市	2008 年 6 月　第二批
119	晋剧（井陉县）	石家庄市	2011 年 5 月　第三批
120	评剧	石家庄市	2011 年 5 月　第三批
121	新乐伏羲祭典	石家庄市	2011 年 5 月　第三批
122	河南坠子（临漳）	邯郸市	2011 年 5 月　第三批
123	梅花拳（威县）	邢台市	2011 年 5 月　第三批
124	固安柳编	廊坊市	2011 年 5 月　第三批
125	八卦掌（固安）	廊坊市	2011 年 5 月　第三批
126	安国老调	保定市	2011 年 5 月　第三批

（续表）

序号	名称	属地	批次
127	直隶官府菜烹饪技艺	保定市	2011年5月 第三批
128	西路梆子	沧州市	2011年5月 第三批
129	六合拳（泊头市）	沧州市	2011年5月 第三批
130	乐亭地秧歌	唐山市	2011年5月 第三批
131	衡水法帖雕版拓印技艺	衡水市	2011年5月 第三批
132	昌黎皮影戏	秦皇岛市	2011年5月 第三批
133	契丹始祖传说	承德市	2011年5月 第三批
134	鬼谷子传说	邯郸市	2014年11月 第四批
135	戳脚	衡水市	2014年11月 第四批
136	京绣	保定市	2014年11月 第四批
137	布糊画	承德市	2014年11月 第四批
138	水陆画	邯郸市	2014年11月 第四批
139	邢窑陶瓷烧制技艺	邢台市	2014年11月 第四批
140	道教音乐（花张蒙道教音乐）	保定市	2014年11月 第四批
141	乱弹（南岩乱弹）	石家庄市	2014年11月 第四批
142	皮影戏（乐亭皮影戏）	唐山市	2014年11月 第四批
143	太极拳（王其和太极拳）	邢台市	2014年11月 第四批
144	景泰蓝制作技艺	廊坊市	2014年11月 第四批
145	传统棉纺织技艺（威县土布纺织技艺）	邢台市	2014年11月 第四批
146	中医诊疗法（中医络病诊疗方法）	石家庄市	2014年11月 第四批
147	中医诊疗法（脏腑推拿疗法）	保定市	2014年11月 第四批
148	中医传统制剂方法	保定市	2014年11月 第四批
149	元宵节（庄户幡会）	承德市	2014年11月 第四批
150	南路丝弦	邢台市	2021年6月 第五批
151	贾氏青萍剑	沧州市	2021年6月 第五批
152	定州缂丝织造技艺	保定市	2021年6月 第五批
153	定兴书画毡制作技艺	保定市	2021年6月 第五批

（续表）

序号	名称	属地	批次
154	小磨香油制作技艺	邯郸市	2021 年 6 月 第五批
155	滦州地秧歌	唐山市	2021 年 6 月 第五批
156	沙河皮影戏	邢台市	2021 年 6 月 第五批
157	乐亭大鼓	唐山市	2021 年 6 月 第五批
158	孙氏太极拳	保定市	2021 年 6 月 第五批
159	饶阳刻铜	衡水市	2021 年 6 月 第五批
160	刘伶醉酒酿造技艺	保定市	2021 年 6 月 第五批
161	清苑传统制香制作技艺	保定市	2021 年 6 月 第五批
162	腰痛宁组方及其药物炮制工艺	承德市	2021 年 6 月 第五批
163	蔚县打树花	张家口市	2021 年 6 月 第五批

附录 4
河北省历史文化名城名镇名村名录

国家级历史文化名城 6 座：

承德、保定、正定、山海关、邯郸、蔚县

省级历史文化名城 6 座：

宣化、涿州、定州、赵县、邢台、大名

国家级历史文化名镇 8 个：

永年区广府镇、峰峰矿区大社镇、涉县固新镇、武安市冶陶镇、武安市伯延镇、井陉县天长镇、蔚县暖泉镇、蔚县代王城镇

国家级历史文化名村 32 个：

涉县偏城镇偏城村、磁县陶泉乡花驼村、武安市午汲镇大贺庄村、武安市石洞乡什里店村、涉县固新镇原曲村、磁县陶泉乡北岔口村、磁县陶泉乡南王庄村

邢台县路罗镇英谈村、沙河市柴关镇王硇村、沙河市册井乡北盆水村、沙河市柴关乡西沟村、沙河市柴关乡绿水池村、邢台县南石门镇崔路村、邢台县路罗镇鱼林沟村、邢台县将军墓镇内阳村、邢台县太子井乡龙化村

井陉县于家乡于家村、井陉县南障城镇大梁江村、井陉县小龙窝村、井陉县南障城镇吕家村

青苑县冉庄镇冉庄村

怀来县鸡鸣驿乡鸡鸣驿村、蔚县涌泉庄乡北方城村、蔚县宋家庄镇上苏庄村、阳原县浮图讲乡开阳村、蔚县南留庄镇南留庄村、蔚县南留庄镇水西堡村、蔚县宋家庄镇宋家庄村、蔚县宋家庄镇大固城村、蔚县涌泉庄乡任家涧村、蔚县涌泉庄乡堡北卜村、怀来县瑞云观乡镇边城村

省级历史文化名镇 16 个：

武安市阳邑镇、肥乡县天台山镇、大名县金滩镇、武安市淑村镇

邢台县皇寺镇、邢台经济开发区沙河城镇

盐山县庆云镇、东光县连镇镇

224

定州市明月店镇

蔚县宋家庄镇、万全县万全镇

丰宁满族自治县凤山镇

霸州市胜芳镇、霸州市信安镇

遵化市马兰峪镇、迁安市建昌营镇

省级历史文化名村 176 个：

邯郸市：涉县河南店镇赤岸村、涉县井店镇王金庄村、涉县关防乡岭底村、涉县关防乡宋家村、涉县关防乡后岩村、邯郸市峰峰矿区界城镇西老鸦峪村、邯郸市永年区永合会镇王边村、邯郸市峰峰矿区和村镇八特村、邯郸市峰峰矿区和村镇刘岗西村、邯郸市峰峰矿区义井镇山底村、涉县更乐镇大洼村、磁县陶泉乡西花园村、磁县陶泉乡齐家岭村、磁县北贾璧乡西苗庄村、磁县北贾璧乡双和村、磁县北贾璧乡岗西村、磁县北贾璧乡柴庄村、磁县白土镇吴家河村、磁县白土镇北羊城村、武安市徘徊镇西河下村、武安市活水乡楼上村、武安市磁山镇明峪村、武安市邑城镇白府村

邢台市：平乡县丰州镇窦冯马村、临城县赵庄乡驾游村、内丘县南赛乡神头村、沙河市十里亭镇上申庄村、沙河市柴关乡安河村、沙河市册井乡册井村、沙河市刘石岗乡大坪村、沙河市刘石岗乡渐凹村、沙河市白塔镇樊下曹村、邢台县南石门镇小桃花村、邢台县黄寺镇李梅花村、邢台县北小庄乡东石善村、邢台县路罗镇桃树坪村、邢台县西黄村镇南会村、内丘县獐獏乡黄岔村、临城县郝庄镇郝庄村、内丘县南赛乡石盆村、内丘县侯家庄乡小西村、沙河市册井乡八十县村、沙河市册井乡白庄村、沙河市册井乡通元井村、沙河市新城镇白错村、沙河市新城镇三王村、沙河市柴关乡柴关村、沙河市柴关乡陈硇村、沙河市柴关乡东沟村、沙河市柴关乡杜硇村、沙河市柴关乡高庄村、沙河市柴关乡马峪村、沙河市柴关乡彭硇村、沙河市柴关乡石门沟村、沙河市柴关乡杏花庄村、沙河市柴关乡银河沟村、沙河市蝉房乡后渐寺村、沙河市蝉房乡渐滩村、沙河市蝉房乡口上村、沙河市蝉房乡前渐寺村、沙河市蝉房乡王茜村、沙河市蝉房乡温家沟村、沙河市蝉房乡小汗坡村、沙河市刘石岗乡寺庄村、沙河市綦村镇城湾村、沙河市綦村镇西南沟村、沙河市十里亭镇下解村、沙河市桥东街道小仓村、邢台市信都区路罗镇杜彬村、邢台市信都区路罗镇牛豆台村、邢台市信都区路罗镇茶旧沟村、邢台市信都区路罗镇小戈寥村、邢台市信都区路罗镇坡子村、邢台市信都区路罗镇杨庄村、邢台市信都区路罗镇贺家坪村、邢台市信都区路罗镇天明关村、邢台市信都区城计头乡押石村、邢台市信都区城计头乡道沟村、邢台市信都区将军墓镇前河岔村、邢台市信都区冀家村乡石板房村、邢台市信都区冀家村乡东庄村、邢台市信都区浆水镇寨上村、邢台市信都区浆水镇菜树沟村、邢台市信都区浆水镇冯家沟村、邢台市信都区浆水镇宋家峪村、邢台市信都区浆水镇前南峪村、邢台市信都区浆水镇安庄村、邢台市信都区浆水镇南口村、邢台市信都区浆水镇坡子峪村

石家庄市：井陉县天长镇梁家村、平山县杨家桥乡大坪村、平山县杨家桥乡大庄村、

井陉县南障城镇小梁江村、井陉县天长镇长生口村、井陉县天长镇核桃园村、井陉县天长镇河东村、井陉县天长镇乏驴岭村、井陉县天长镇板桥村、井陉县天长镇高家庄村、井陉县测鱼镇石门村、井陉县于家乡当泉村、井陉县于家乡狼窝村、井陉县于家乡高家坡村、井陉县于家乡水窑洼村、井陉县南峪镇地都村、井陉县南峪镇南峪村、井陉县小作镇沙窑村、井陉县威州镇北平望村、井陉县秀林镇南横口村、井陉县辛庄乡洪河漕村、井陉县苍岩山镇杨庄村、井陉县南峪镇台头村、石家庄市井陉矿区贾庄镇贾庄村、平山县北冶乡黄安村、平山县古月镇观南庄村、平山县杨家桥乡九里铺村

衡水市： 献县南河头乡单桥村

保定市： 顺平县腰山镇南腰山村、唐县倒马关乡倒马关村、保定市清苑区阎庄乡国公营村、顺平县台鱼乡北康关村、阜平县龙泉关镇骆驼湾村、阜平县天生桥镇朱家庵村、唐县军城镇和家庄村、唐县齐家佐乡史家佐村、涞水县九龙镇岭南台村

定州市： 定州市赵村镇孟家庄村

张家口市： 蔚县代王城镇石家庄村、蔚县宋家庄镇邢家庄村、蔚县宋家庄镇吕家庄村、蔚县宋家庄镇郑家庄村、蔚县涌泉庄乡涌泉庄村、蔚县代王城镇张中堡村、蔚县南留庄镇水东堡村、蔚县宋家庄镇邀渠村、蔚县宋家庄镇南方城村、蔚县宋家庄镇王良庄村、蔚县宋家庄镇北口村、蔚县宋家庄镇大探口村、蔚县西合营镇北留庄村、蔚县西合营镇横涧村、蔚县下宫村乡东庄头村、蔚县下宫村乡浮图村、蔚县下宫村乡苏贾堡村、蔚县阳眷镇南堡村、蔚县阳眷镇郑家窑村、蔚县涌泉庄乡西陈家涧村、蔚县涌泉庄乡辛庄村、蔚县涌泉庄乡闫家寨村、蔚县白草村乡白草村、蔚县白草村乡钟楼村、蔚县柏树乡永宁寨村、蔚县北水泉镇南柏山村、蔚县北水泉镇杨庄村、蔚县代王城镇大德庄村、蔚县代王城镇马家寨村、蔚县南留庄镇白宁堡村、蔚县南留庄镇白中堡村、蔚县南留庄镇曹疃村、蔚县南留庄镇白河东村、蔚县南留庄镇白后堡村、蔚县南留庄镇单堠村、蔚县南留庄镇杜杨庄村、蔚县南留庄镇坞串堡村、蔚县南留庄镇史家堡村、蔚县南留庄镇小饮马泉村、蔚县南杨庄乡东大云疃村、蔚县南杨庄乡牛大人庄村、蔚县暖泉镇千字村、涿鹿县卧佛寺乡狼窝村、涿鹿县大堡镇三道沟村

唐山市： 遵化市马兰峪镇官房村、遵化市马兰峪镇马兰关一村、遵化市新店子镇沙石峪村、遵化市建明镇西铺村

秦皇岛市： 抚宁区界岭口村

References
参考文献

［1］陈正祥. 中国历史文化地理 [M]. 太原：山西人民出版社，2021.

［2］胡克夫. 燕赵文化丛书 [M]. 石家庄：河北教育出版社，2016.

［3］黄仁宇. 中国大历史 [M]. 北京：生活・读书・新知三联书店，2021.

［4］康金莉. 大运河河北段历史文化记忆 [M]. 北京：北京师范大学出版社，2021.

［5］梁思成. 中国建筑史 [M]. 北京：生活・读书・新知三联书店，2011.

［6］桑献凯，曹征平，王宁. 大河之北 [M]. 石家庄：花山文艺出版社，2021.

［7］王智. 燕赵传奇 [M]. 石家庄：河北教育出版社，2015.

［8］许倬云. 中国文化的精神 [M]. 北京：九州出版社，2021.

［9］郑绍宗. 河北古长城 [M]. 石家庄：河北教育出版社，2016.